Collusive Strangers

Selected Publications by Jeremy Reed
indicates a Shearsman publication

Poetry
The Isthmus of Samuel Greenberg (1976; 2nd edition 2018*)
Bleecker Street (1980)
By the Fisheries (1984)
Nero (1985)
Selected Poems (1987)
Engaging Form (1988)
Nineties (1990)
Red Haired Android (1992)
Kicks (1994)
Pop Stars, with Mick Rock (1995)
Sweet Sister Lyric (1996)
Saint Billie (2000)
Patron Saint of Eyeliner (2000)
Heartbreak Hotel (2002)
Duck and Sally Inside (2006)
Orange Sunshine (2006)
This Is How You Disappear (2007)
West End Survival Kit (2009)
Bona Drag (2009)*
Black Russian: Out-takes from the Airmen's Club 1978-9 (2010)
Piccadilly Bongo (with Marc Almond) (2010)
Bona Vada (2011)*
Whitehall Jackals (with Chris McCabe) (2013)
The Glamour Poet… (2014)*
Sooner or Later Frank (2014)
Shakespeare in Soho (2017)
Psychedelic Meadow (2019)

Novels
The Lipstick Boys (1984)
Blue Rock (1987)
Red Eclipse (1989)
Inhabiting Shadows (1990)
Isidore (1991)
When The Whip Comes Down (1992)
Chasing Black Rainbows (1994)
The Pleasure Chateau (1994)
Diamond Nebula (1995)
Red Hot Lipstick (1996)
Sister Midnight (1997)
Dorian (1998)
Boy Caesar (2004)
The Grid (2008)
Here Comes the Nice (2011)

Collusive Strangers
New Selected Poems

Jeremy Reed

Edited with an Introduction by Grevel Lindop

Shearsman Books

First published in the United Kingdom in 2024 by
Shearsman Books Ltd
PO Box 4239
Swindon
SN3 9FN

Shearsman Books Ltd Registered Office
30–31 St. James Place, Mangotsfield, Bristol BS16 9JB
(this address not for correspondence)

ISBN 978-1-84861-915-9

Introduction copyright © Grevel Lindop, 2024

Poems copyright © 1979–2016 by Jeremy Reed.
The right of Jeremy Reed to be identified as the author of this
work has been asserted by him in accordance with the
Copyrights, Designs and Patents Act of 1988.
All rights reserved.

CONTENTS

Acknowledgements	13
Introduction by Grevel Lindop	15

From *Saints and Psychotics* (1979)

To Have and Have Not	27
Bankrupt	28
Liquidation	29
Throttling the Pilot	30

From *Black Russian: Outtakes from the Airmen's Club 1978–9* (2010)

[*from*] Junky Tango Outside Boot's Piccadilly [stanzas 16-22]	31
Claustrophobia (Kings Cross)	33

From *Bleecker Street* (1980)

Reading You Rilke	34
Face to the Wall	35
In the Chair	36
Metallic	37
A Jump in the Picture	38
Three Devils Reef	39
Visit to George Barker	40
Marlowe's Letter to Thomas Walsingham	42

From *A Long Shot to Heaven* (1982)

Late One	46
John Clare's Journal	47
Dwight's Brother	50
Cartford	53
Adam	55

From *A Man Afraid* (1982):

On Arrival	56
Sweet Jar	57
Parallel Orange	58

From *By the Fisheries* (1984):

By the Fisheries	59
Composition	61
Christopher Smart in Madness	62
Housman in Old Age	65
Rifts	66
Visiting Hours	68
Lumber Room	70
Conger	71
Air	73
Stick by Stick	75
Dead Hand	77
The Storm	79

From *Nero* (1985)

Spider Fire	81
Dead Weasels	83
Winter Mullet	85
Ants	87
The Wake's Departure	89
Baudelaire in Middle Age	90
Heirloom	92
Regular	94
Nero	96
Late Year Fog	100

From *The Escaped Image* (1988)

Houses We Never Live In	102

From *Engaging Form* (1988)

Marbles	103
My Father's Models	104
Bugging	106
Pond Skaters	107
Fermentation	108
An Old Score	109
Space Facilitator	110
Terrorists	111
Blue Lagoon	112
Farmdog	113
A Visit	114
Changes	116
Crows in a Misty Field	118
Elm Load	119
Moth-trapper	121
The Grand Tour	122
Pacts	124
Elder Wine	125

From *Dicing for Pearls* (1990)

Babel	127

From *Nineties* (1990)

All the President's Men	128
AIDS	130
Love and Death	131
Invisible Cities	132
Flaubert	133
Snake Fight	135
Bathroom Scene	137
Blueprint	138
Samaritans	139
Transsexual	140
Brothels	141

Revocation	142
The Various Ways	143
Cézanne	144
Discoveries	146
After It Was Over	147
Mistletoe	148
Standing Off	149
Prayer	151

From *Red-Haired Android* (1992)

Stardust	153
After the Great Discoveries	154
Madonna	155
Dusting the Arm-Rest	157
Keepers of the Night	158
Detoxification	159
Jays	160
Graffiti Artist	161
George	162
Arsonist	163
Letters	164
Toad	166
Clearance	167
De Sade	168
The Catch in the Stairs	170
Between the 3rd and 5th	171
Undercurrents	172
The Unexpected Lesson	174
Archival	175
The New Age	176

From *Black Sugar* (1992)

Hey	177
Black Sugar	178
Transvestites	179

From *Pop Stars* (1995)

Elvis Presley	180
Marc Bolan	181
Rock and Poetry	182

From *Saint Billie* (2000)

Loving that Man of Mine	184

From *Heartbreak Hotel* (2002)

The Colonel's Machinations	185
The Sixties	187
Junk-food Junkie	189
Divorce	190

From *Duck and Sally Inside* (2004)

Looking Out (Looking at You)	192
Penguin Modern Classics	193
The Futures	195
Lapsang Souchong	197
Elegy for David Gascoyne	198
Nifty Jim	201
Re-reading Sylvia Plath	202
Talkin' 'Bout Regeneration	204
Peonies	206
Danish Pastry	208
Marina	209
Cold Fog	211

From *Orange Sunshine* (2006)

Edith Grove	213
Regent Sound	215

Cecil Beaton Photographs Jagger	217
Elegy for a Polka Dot Shirt	219
Swinging London	220
The Dealer	222
Mods	223
The Merseybeats	225

From *This Is How You Disappear* (2007)

Asa Benveniste	226
Mary Absalom	228
Paula Stratton	230
John Berger	233

From *West End Survival Kit* (2009)

Mercy	239
West End Survival Kit	241
Altered Geography	243
Smart Pill	245
The Reckoning	247
Yukio-Joe and Princess Di	249
Drug Giant PA	251

From *Bona Drag* (2009)

Jaffa Cakes	253
Vertigo	254
The Future Arrived Too Early	256
Tipping Points	258

From *Piccadilly Bongo* (2010)

Piccadilly Bongo	259
30 Bedford Square	261

Why I Hate Poetry	263
Chrysanthemums	264
Yellow Irises	265
Jersey Breakfast	267

From *Whitehall Jackals* (2013)

Fleet	269
Yauatcha	271
Shoplifting at Selfridges	272
The Right Hon. Jackal Blair	274
London Flowers	275

From *Living the Blues* (2014)

South End Green Toilets, NW3	276

From *Nothing But a Star* (2014)

Workshop	277
Pulling the Cork	278
Maddox Street	279
Elegy for Paul Lightborn	280
Shares	282
Hanging On	283
Charles Baudelaire, Voyage to Cythera – (Sex Tourist Remix)	285

From *Sooner or Later Frank* (2014)

Peter's Lay Out	287
M&S Socks	288
Rainbow Country	290
Starbucks Pitch	292
Honey	293

Buying Cup Cakes	294
Death Date Cutie	295
My Death Shirt	296
Hart Crane's Jump	298

From *The Glamour Poet Versus Francis Bacon,
Rent and Eyelinered Pussycat Dolls* (2014)

from White Bear and Francis Bacon	299

From *Voodoo Excess* (2015)

Keith Richards	303
Ronnie Wood	304

From *Red Light Blues* (2016)

Some Day	305

ACKNOWLEDGEMENTS

I am grateful to all those who have helped to make this Selection possible, not least to those publishers and editors who have granted permission for me to include poems first published under their imprints. My thanks for such permissions go to Tony Frazer at Shearsman Books; to Andrew Duncan and Simon Jenner at Waterloo Press; and to Stephen Stuart-Smith at Enitharmon Editions. Other poems published here are the copyright of Jeremy Reed.

Stephen Stuart-Smith gave invaluable help by lending volumes of Jeremy Reed's work; by arranging to have many early poems from pre-computer days typed for inclusion; and by supplying complete digital files of several later books.

Jeremy Reed not only authorised the selection but supported it with constantly stimulating and revelatory letters, and the gift of numerous out-of-print and limited editions which would otherwise have escaped me.

I need hardly say how grateful I am to Tony Frazer for his willingness to take on a project which might well have daunted less adventurous publishers. By doing so he has left us more deeply than ever indebted for his services to the poetry of our times.

First publishers of the volumes drawn on here were as follows:
Cape: *By the Fisheries* (1984), *Nero* (1985), *Engaging Form* (1988);
Carcanet Press: *Bleecker Street* (1980);
Chomu Press: *Nothing But a Star* (2014);
City Lights: *Red-Haired Android* (1993);
Enitharmon Press/Enitharmon Editions: *Saints and Psychotics* (1979), *A Man Afraid* (1982), *Dicing for Pearls* (1990), *Pop Stars* (1995), *Saint Billy* (2000), *Duck and Sally Inside* (2004), *This Is How You Disappear* (2007), *Piccadilly Bongo* (2010), *Sooner or Later Frank* (2014), *Voodoo Excess* (2015);
The Menard Press: *A Long Shot to Heaven* (1982);
Nine Arches: *Whitehall Jackals* (2013);
Orion: *Heartbreak Hotel* (2002);
Peter Owen: *Black Sugar* (1992);
Publication Studio: *Living the Blues* (2014);
SAF Publishing: *Orange Sunshine*;
Shearsman Books: *Bona Drag* (2009), *The Glamour Poet versus Francis Bacon, Rent and Eyelinered Pussycat Dolls* (2014);

The Society Club: *Red Light Blues* (2016);
Vintage: *Nineties* (1990);
Waterloo Press: *West End Survival Kit* (2009), *Black Russian: Outtakes from the Airmen's Club, 1978–9* (2010);
Words Press: *The Escaped Image* (1988).

Grevel Lindop
2024

INTRODUCTION

For years I've been hoping to edit a substantial selection of Jeremy Reed's poems. Here it is at last. I offer it for two main reasons. The first is sheer enthusiasm. Having followed Reed's work over many years, I've never failed to come away from it with sharpened perceptions of the world and an enhanced sense of the marvels language can perform. But my second reason is a realisation that readers urgently need a map to the work of the most prolific, and perhaps the most remarkable poet of his generation.

Jeremy Reed's output has been prodigious. Since 1975 he has published more than forty books of poems, besides countless pamphlets and fugitive pieces, and many novels, biographies and books on cultural history. The full range of his poetry will never be truly known, for he often writes in public places, and if someone expresses interest may give them the poem. By the time this selection appears his tally will have grown further, because he writes continuously. His poems are his diary, his autobiography, his therapy, his addiction. Reed has moved from publisher to publisher, often writing for several at the same time, and his style has evolved continuously over more than four decades. Formalist, symbolist, language poet, nature-poet, modernist, post-modernist, performance poet: Reed has been all these and more.

So who is Jeremy Reed, and why is his work important? He was born in 1951 in Jersey, and educated there and at Essex University. Since finishing postgraduate work at Essex, he has lived mainly as a freelance writer, with all the determination and insecurity that implies. His origins may have some bearing on his work. Jersey is much closer to France than to England; it's probably no accident that Reed's early affinities were with the European Symbolists: he completely bypassed the drab 'Movement' poetry which dominated (and still influences) British writing. Possibly the same factor contributed to Reed's permanent sense of being an outsider in British society. His observation is the heightened, angular vision of someone who doesn't fit in. His models have been rebels and creative misfits: Rimbaud, Baudelaire, Blake, Aragon, Wilde, Hart Crane. His first book, indeed, was *The Isthmus of Samuel Greenberg* (1976), a sequence inspired by the self-taught, poverty-stricken poet whose work gave Hart Crane the basis for several major poems.

I've chosen to open this selection, though, with 'To Have and Have Not', a marvellous short poem from 1979 that shows many of Reed's defining qualities: vivid colour-imagery; staccato sentences; syntax clipped to a minimum in defiance of grammatical decorum; and above all a pervasive dynamism. Pitting opposites against each other, the poem generates tension like a coiled spring. A quintessential Symbolist experience, it forces us to read again and again in an effort to resolve contradictions which refuse to settle. As the poem asks (or states: typically, there is no question mark) 'how on a spiritual plane unite / the blues of ectoplasm.' Deadly serious from the start, Reed's poetry is also invariably playful; you can lose yourself in a poem like this for a long time. Other poems from the same early collection, *Saints and Psychotics*, display his debts to Surrealism ('Liquidation'), and the thriller genre ('Throttling the Pilot'). The latter introduces the first of many sinister treatments of airliners, always an ominous image in Reed's work; he has admitted in an interview that he is 'aviophobic' and dislikes long-haul flights. Watch out for the aircraft overhead in several of his poems.

These early poems also reveal another key quality: Reed's immense vocabulary. Already this handful of early poems offers 'trichromatic', 'paraldehyde', 'maelstromic', 'cumulose', 'annihilative', 'sense-querulous'. Vertigo is a 'syringe-head'; altitude 'fog-snakes'; smog is 'siamese-beige'. Reed has always used language with such restlessness, splicing words into startling compounds, welcoming malformations, misspellings and malapropisms, ransacking chemistry, neurology, electronics, astronomy and fashion for new vocabulary. In later poems we shall meet 'necrogenes', 'erinyes', 'coppled', 'psychopannichysmic' and many more. This constant excitement about language is inseparable from the impatient fertility of his work.

The 2010 volume, *Black Russian: Outtakes from the Airmen's Club 1978–9*, is an extreme example of the winding paths Reed's work can take before it finds itself in print. The manuscript was apparently lost to sight for some forty years. It surfaced to be published in 2010 by Waterloo Press, but as far as I can tell only a single review appeared (by Mark Wilson, at thefiendjournal.wordpress.com) and the book has remained almost unnoticed. This is the more astonishing because it contains what I believe to be one of the twentieth century's great poems, 'Junky Tango Outside Boot's Piccadilly', an elegy for Reed's friend Paula Stratton, a heroin addict who took her own life. In 688 lines (86 stanzas of eight lines each), the poem draws on ancient Egyptian funerary customs, the cabbala, the Tarot, the geography of London (the Tube featuring vividly, as often in Reed's poems) and it flickers with extraordinary visions. Paula 'fear[ed] a hospital / more than a crab pincering its caged-pot'; her friends panic 'like a blind goat, / its eyes sewn up in the burial-pit'; outside the room, 'a brown-eyed night wind / felt in the ash tree for your body's parts'. I should have liked to include the whole of this remarkable poem, but only a sample can be given. I urge the reader to seek it out.

Reed's apparent nonchalance in neglecting this magnificent work seems inexplicable. Presumably his relentless focus on the next poem or project simply led him to move on without making sustained efforts to publish it. His 1980 volume *Bleecker Street* (named for Hart Crane's address in Manhattan) contains a variety of short poems ranging from the near-social realism of 'Face to the Wall' ('January: the old no longer / retrieve mail from an unheated / hall') by way of the classic Symbolism of 'Reading You Rilke' to 'In the Chair', a disturbing, surreal vignette probably inspired by the punishment meted out by the Kray twins to an associate. 'Metallic', which explores the poet's cringing allergy one day to metallic things ('how they arrive with the wince of [dental] fillings'), offers one clue to Reed's astonishing poetic fertility, in his readiness to explore private and irrational experiences – the kind of thing most people would simply dismiss as bizarre subjective distractions – and find pattern and meaning in them. More expansively, the collection includes the conversational 'Visit to George Barker' – both an alluring pastoral and a tribute to a poetic influence – and 'Marlowe's Letter to Thomas Walsingham', where the letter's actual purport is almost indiscernible beyond the pyrotechnic displays of Elizabethan urban imagery. Not surprisingly, given his copious vocabulary and the creative panache of his use (and creative misuse) of language, Reed has felt an enduring affinity with the Elizabethans, facets of which later included a complete modern rewriting of Shakespeare's sonnets (as *The Billy Boy Remixes*, 2016) and a 2008 novel, *The Grid*, which imagines Marlowe as a screenwriter in a dystopian twenty-first century London. 'The Queen beats like a black swan on Lethe' is a line Marlowe himself would have admired.

'Dwight's Brother', from *A Long Shot to Heaven* (1982), introduces another facet of Reed's creative vision: science-fiction poems, in which he relishes creating a dystopian vision, applying his gift for hyper-realistic description (the sky is 'a bubble policed by piranha'; drugs turn brain cells 'into a ziggurat / of future galaxies') to studies of paranoia and what he calls, in a phrase of classical exactness, 'the monomania that burns planets'. 'Cartford' offers one of Reed's characteristically skewed narratives, where a country clergyman, oblivious of the crashed light aircraft exploding in the nearby wood, runs from his house in terror; but terror of what? 'Clare's Journal' speaks for another outsider poet, the 'mad' Northamptonshire peasant John Clare, sharing with him the acute observation that powers so many of Reed's own nature poems: 'for three minutes I've timed / a snail's progress over a slender spar / of twig.' Even the word 'spar' is just right, and one that probably no other poet would have hit on.

Those nature poems came into their own spectacularly with *By the Fisheries*, the magnificent 1984 volume which gained universal acclaim from reviewers, headed by Seamus Heaney, and won Reed the Somerset Maugham Award the following year. Its needle-sharp descriptive skills, based on an almost fanatically close observation of the natural world – Reed is a skilled fisherman and a deeply knowledgeable naturalist – bombard the mind's eye with glistening images which generate continual pleasure. An ivy-leaf after rain is 'a diamond-lit frog's back'; a woodlouse 'locks fast in the log's slow rot'; on a lake, 'web-footed duck wakes…cut the green silk to a convict's cloth / of arrows.' Other poems, such as the compassionate, emotionally raw 'Visiting Hours', touch a confessional note close to (but more musical than) Robert Lowell's: 'I see my own death frozen in a beam, / as it will isolate me years later, / And I without offspring. You are my son / in these last weeks…. I too fear the end of visiting hours.' *By the Fisheries* is probably the best starting-point for a reader completely new to Jeremy Reed.

The brilliant evocations of animals, insects, and landscapes – alongside explorations of alienated decadence – continued through *Nero* (1985) and *Engaging Form* (1988). The common denominator is intensity: for a splendid example see 'Spider Fire' where a wildfire is viewed both in close-up ('the tenacious marauding wolf-spider / running across hairline fissures') and from afar, where the fire's trace becomes 'a black hoop ironed into the landscape'. On a different scale, 'Marbles' is one of many poems scattered through Reed's oeuvre in which he rejoices in small colourful objects ('the opalescent whites, a twist / of scarlet in crystal'). To enjoy other examples, see 2004's 'Danish Pastry', and (from 2014) 'M&S Socks' and 'Buying Cup-Cakes'.

But by 1990, celebrating the new decade explicitly in *Nineties*, Reed was growing tired of being known simply as a 'nature poet' – though this very volume contains the gorgeously traditional 'Mistletoe', and he has never abandoned the natural world: flowers have remained a recurrent subject of sensuous celebration. Sometime during the preceding decade he had moved to London (though for a poet so self-revealing in detail, the broad outlines of Reed's biography are remarkably hard to establish). Darker, more disturbing themes were pressing in on him – above all the AIDS epidemic. The poem 'AIDS' itself fascinatingly shows the nature-images ('first mauve crocuses' and a coast 'lavender as the shower moves in') now grasped-at as evasion and consolation, when the poet spots a 'friend of my youth, iller, older' and 'won't enquire' because of the likely answer. 'All the President's Men' applies his gift for dystopian sci-fi to political satire: continents nuked while politicians drink champagne. This seems also to have been a dark time for Reed personally: the immensely brave 'Samaritans' puts us in the telephone booth with the caller clawing his way back from the edge of suicide (again the 'lobster-pot' image); and 'Prayer', an explicitly religious poem of a kind Reed has never written, so far as I know, before or since, is a magnificent *cri de cœur* which would demand a place in any anthology of religious poetry but seems, like most of Reed's work, to have been unaccountably forgotten.

Red-Haired Android (1992) – a book of 280 pages, as long as many poets' collected works – continued Reed's self-transformation. As the book's title suggests, there are more sci-fi poems. A keynote poem, 'The New Age', announces 'We're in it, and it's caught us unawares', and goes on to ask 'How can I direct poetry / towards the future's disconnected images / that flash by on a filmic screen? ... We're all in each other's film and conscious of that, / live through the imitative and not the real.' Written in or before 1992, this is deeply prophetic. 'Detoxification' implies drug-withdrawal, opening with more than a hint of prayer: 'So help me purify / whatever new cells will regenerate / my clean blood at the end of it,' in a struggle to break 'the cycle's remorseless continuity, / the chemical's biography / controlling mine.' The drug, in a reminiscence perhaps of Nerval's 'Soleil noir de la Mélancolie', is 'my black inner chemical sun.' The volume also contains, in 'Madonna', one of the first of Reed's poems about pop stars, a theme destined to become of great importance in his work. It opens, significantly, with the line 'It's all a question of identity,' and this is indeed the key: for Reed the self-presentation of pop stars, the treatment of the body, and the life, as confrontational cultural icons inseparable from the words and the music, would become the crucial instance of contemporary social reality and aesthetics: fascinating and problematic because diametrically opposite to the spontaneous yet fixed life of what we call nature.

Another recurring strand notable in the 1992 book is that of the poem about poetry. 'Dusting the Arm-Rest' begins, unforgettably, 'Poetry is a wolf watching the world', and ends 'imparting a savage dementia / to the one waiting for it in the dark.' This – poetry as a kind of rabies – is not a comfortable view; and indeed, few Reed volumes have appeared without, somewhere, a poem making clear his opinions on poetry, which are anything but anodyne. As early as *Bleecker Street*, he had denounced 'the malaise of English poetry, that vacillates; / and so, is circumscribed to the ephemeral.' ('Visit to George Barker'). His views, if anything, have intensified since then: a typical comment from a 2010 interview (in the journal *London Calling*) was 'The mainstream bore me, they're 19th Century, and they're still writing about the 1950s; all that Simon Armitage, Andrew Motion crap to me belongs to a sort of E. M. Forster generation.... they're dead to almost everything that's happening around them... I think English poetry will always be fifty years behind the times.' In this book I have included, also from 2010, 'Why I Hate Poetry', a magnificent tirade which begins 'I prefer Maltesers to poetry'.

It was with *Pop Stars* (1995), a book of poems with photographs by Mick Rock, that Reed's concern with the pop world came into its own. Alongside the questions of aesthetics and psychology raised by popular culture, another facet of Reed's interest now becomes clear, which is that he wants poetry to have the same energy as pop: 'speed injected into words, / the volatile flash lifting syllables / into a rain forest of coloured birds.' Poetry, in fact, 'needs street-cred, an energy / vital to youth'. Reed's own work as a performance poet and collaborator with pop musicians has sought to embody this, but it was not a view likely to endear him to the poetic establishment. In the Anglophone regions (unlike the French and Hispanic) the realms of pop music and poetry are regarded as worlds apart and view each other with mutual contempt. A few licensed exceptions apart (Nick Cave, Leonard Cohen, Bob Dylan), anyone trying to bridge the gap is dismissed with scorn. Reed was on dangerous ground. As he moved further from the familiar realm of nature poetry to write about AIDS and drug abuse, attack the poetry establishment, and look to the pop world for inspiration, he was regarded, in some quarters, with increasing hostility. He compounded his crimes in 2002 with *Heartbreak Hotel*, an entire book of poems tracing the life of Elvis Presley. *Heartbreak Hotel* is perhaps too long, with some repetition and redundancy. But it is astonishingly original and contains some splendid poems. Its view of Presley as a martyr to his own garish success is both compassionate and scathing, as the quintessential pop star, a naïve prisoner to his manager, gawps, drug-fuddled and uncomprehending, at the 1960s world he has helped to create. 'Junk-Food Junkie' is a hilarious, magnificent and appalling Rabelaisian paean to the achievements of a compulsive eater in junk food hell. Reed would return to his exploration of pop in *Orange Sunshine* (2006), a full-length book of poems about the 1960s with a sustained focus on the music, its studio production, and its social context; and in *Voodoo Excess* (2015), which collected, with many new additions, his poems about the Rolling Stones. This strand of his work reached its apotheosis in 2010's *Piccadilly Bongo*, a book of poems issued with a CD of songs by Marc Almond and prefaced by Almond himself.

With *Duck and Sally Inside* (2004) Reed began regular publication with Enitharmon Press. His debut with his new publisher is one of his finest books, and another excellent starting-point for those new to his work. Its poems cover almost the full span of Reed's concerns up to that point: major figures are assessed, with poems about David Gascoyne (a personal friend) and 'Re-Reading Sylvia Plath' – the latter beginning, characteristically, 'I don't do literature, but…'; bizarre, gender-bending sci-fi glamour is imagined in 'The Futures'; 'Peonies' – one I have picked from a whole garden of flower-poems that stud the original collection – combines superb description ('carmine extravaganzas / like a Galliano hat / ice-cream scooped with ruffles') with uneasy autobiography; there are the wonderful, Turneresque London skyscapes Reed does so well ('The year's obit is fluffy with blue stuff / poured from a smoky opalescent sky / the sunrise back of it an orange block / smudged out by particle glitter'). And there are quite unexpected pleasures. The determinedly non-literary Reed writes a celebration of 'Penguin Modern Classics'; the tough-talking decadent offers the most delicate and compassionate portraits of individuals in all their quirky particularity: 'Nifty Jim' who ends up reduced to a cruel headline, 'man in red lipstick stole for kicks'; 'Marina', the 'puckishly vivacious' Croatian waitress who 'injected upbeat tempo / into our café, … singing back-up chorus to / the radio' and is sadly missed. Perhaps the most extraordinary poem is 'Looking Out (Looking at You)' which presents an evanescent, momentary romantic encounter – just a glance between the poet and a girl in a café – entirely in terms of demographic classification, much of it by means of brand names. The girl (like the poet) is 'one in twelve million in the London grid', classified as: 'age 25? Nationality / Hispanic? blood type O? hair hennaed red?' –

> her blue nail polish (Bourjois?) eyeliner
> a cobalt (No. 17?), black jeans
> label hidden, a sassy (D&G?),
> grey cashmere jumper (Jigsaw?), black bra-strap
> a pointy (Gossard Wonderbra?)
> big-screen sunglasses (Boots or a Drugstore?)

The poem, of fascinating originality, goes to the heart of the way people are currently enmeshed – almost shredded – by a predetermined range of manufactured choices. Yet the girl remains resolutely individual – she has a copy of Nietzsche's *Zarathustra* in her bag – and the poem remains romantic, celebrating the possibility of a relationship, glimpsed and lost. Add to this 'Lapsang Souchong', the finest poem you are ever likely to read about tea – Reed is the laureate of tea: he has written about it several times (see the 2013 'Yauatcha' for another example) – and you will begin to understand my enthusiasm for *Duck and Sally*.

Reed has always been a great writer of elegies, and in *This Is How You Disappear* (2007) he returned to the *genre* with panache. The dead friends celebrated include the avant-garde poet-publisher Asa Benveniste, who had published Reed's early work through his Trigram Press imprint and whom we shall meet again in 2014's *The Glamour Poet*; the unforgotten Paula Stratton, celebrated long ago in *Junky Tango*; and, in a searingly colourful and vivid elegy, John Berger: not the writer, but the larger-than-life heir to the Berger paint fortune, a Jersey resident and early mentor to the poet. Incestuous, a Nazi sympathiser during the Jersey occupation, Berger is presented without judgment and stands out in all his bizarre glory, an irreducible individual, even after his death (which Reed describes) and his cremation 'to clean ash'. I'm not sure there's a character-sketch to match this anywhere in contemporary poetry.

As the twenty-first century moved on, an unexpected facet started to show itself in Reed's work: the political. Something of the kind had always been latent in his dystopian fantasies, with their horror of totalitarian violence. Now the vision, however futuristic, closes in on contemporary history. 'Yukio-Joe and Princess Di' from *West End Survival Kit* imagines the Princess 'back again / dodging CCTV at Harvey Nicks, / her face retooled after the crash, her brain still part amnesiac'. Shoplifting, hallucinating, 'She's got it bad, withdrawal from fame.' It was the Blair years, their reckless military interventions justified by obvious lies and resulting in countless deaths and failed-state chaos, that provoked Reed into his bitterest writing. In *Whitehall Jackals*, where Jeremy Reed and Chris McCabe contributed poems on alternate pages, Reed subjected Blair and his companions to the vicious caricature of a Swift or a Hogarth. Blair, the 'globe-trotting criminal', is 'Insensitive as a mortuary fridge,' with 'a jackal's / asymmetrically psychopathic grin'. In his world, 'people stick like eggs to a pan / fried by depleted uranium'. The vision is extended in 2014's 'Charles Baudelaire, Voyage to Cythera – (Sex Tourist Remix)', where

French Symbolist foundations (with recollections of 'Une charogne' as well as of 'Un voyage à Cythère') support the vision of a dismembered Blair treated like the many victims of his war, while the closing rhyme of the last quatrain clinches an ending so powerful I won't spoil it by quoting it here. Meanwhile, the restless quest for new subjects went on as ever. From *Living the Blues*, a rare volume from Publication Studio of Portland, Oregon, I'm delighted to present 'South End Green Toilets, NW3'. Many poems, good and bad, have been written *in* such establishments; this is, as far as I know, the only fully-accomplished poem to have been written *about* one.

In 2014 Jeremy Reed published the first results of an entirely new enterprise: a long autobiographical poem. *The Glamour Poet versus Francis Bacon, Rent and Eyelinered Pussycat Dolls* consists largely of 'White Bear   and Francis Bacon' (the white space in the title apparently intentional), which meditates, amongst other topics less prominently treated, on Bacon's use of colour (the artist had been Reed's occasional patron during the 1980s) and on the poet's recollections – confirmed by his social history *The Dilly* – of working at times as a Piccadilly rent boy. The poem – some 4,500 lines long – is, Reed claims, merely 'the first book of my long London poem'. One would expect that a poem of such ambition, by a highly literate and technically skilled poet, dealing with the sex industry from personal experience, might have attracted *some* attention from mainstream cultural commentators. But as far as I can discover, no literary critic, no poetry blogger, no sociologist or psychologist, not even a single *journalist*, wrote about the book.

All I can do here is offer two extracts. The first is Reed's profoundly compassionate recollection of 'Alfie', an unforgettable portrait of a man in terminal despair to whom the poet can afford no solace but listening. I've had to cut the passage (the original sentence is 166 words) so the lack of final punctuation is intended. I follow this with an extract from Reed's account of a meeting with Asa Benveniste, one of his first publishers, in Jersey. It's a passage that epitomises so many of Reed's accomplishments: the sharp character-sketch (Benveniste 'spaghetti-thin, black-shirted'); the unabashed celebration of food (potatoes 'tangy like seaweed … blotchy ovoids flipped like black gold out of the April soil'); the astonishingly fertile tossing up of superb nature-imagery ('an oak's twisted torso'; 'crows conven[ing] with their dodgy runic vocabulary') that's nonetheless spiked with awareness of how pastoral has been penetrated by corporate greed: 'a Chinese puzzle of lanes / with sunken farms and manors sealed like forts / into a video-alert / motion-sensored plutocracy'. The freshness of Reed's language and vision is untarnished.

I end this selection with 2016's 'Some Day', a suitably retrospective poem movingly conjuring scenes and people from the past, and offering a poignant glimpse of the poet's mother, who has rarely appeared in his work. Its closing image – 'a broken rainbow / over my backyard that won't disappear' – is as good an emblem as any for Reed's extraordinary work.

I've chosen this book's title from several offered by Jeremy Reed himself. I hope it catches the sense of random yet meaningful connection, of rich incongruity and guilty pleasure which often typify his poetry. The poems I've chosen will be strangers to most of my readers; but I hope that, once introduced, readers and poems will collaborate, collude, co-operate and cross-fertilise to bring delight, enlightenment and an appetite for more. I could easily have made a selection far larger than this one, and written much more about it. Especially I regret having said nothing about form and prosody; I assume that the variety of forms on display in this book will speak for itself. But space is limited and what matters is the poetry. Jeremy, meanwhile, is far ahead of us, writing as always. Time to get reading, or we'll be left behind.

Grevel Lindop

TO HAVE AND HAVE NOT

Reclusive, I painted the house-exterior
white, interior black.
Exorcised the mundane red of my cells,
roses grew on the track.

The reverse of myself acquainted with
a globe and itinerary,
erased my past, and my future passport
to, from identity.

And then the two selves met at a junction,
could not exchange salutation,
nor concede rights to whom was secular.
Division called for an ocean.

But how on a spiritual plane unite
the blues of ectoplasm.
One weather the rain a white headstone, one
black in the frock of cremation.

BANKRUPT

In childhood his kite was
trichromatic, self-
levitated above the grass,
paper-crisp, daring rarer vapours,
a continuity
of the sky's colour. And
in later life, (opulence
acquired by inheritance)
his hand guided the paper's
rectangle, to an escalator
windowed with furnished cells,
ascending by storey and street
until his apex was concrete
and the rents inordinately steep
by step.
                But the kite
rose to the syringe-head of vertigo,
inveighed with by condors
striking blood for their mint, and height
assumed without faculty.
Lines on the paper descended obliquely,
the rooms untenanted;
and he lay again unconscious of weight
on the grass with his kite
red on the bullet side of transparency.

LIQUIDATION

Sits on. The walls reflect a black canal
which fluctuates like an anaesthetic
that's undispelled, and then that stagnant thirst
that rouses him from a cane piano-stool
to circle violet light.
                      'Another tangent now,
those bottles of paraldehyde, and rails
conveying distance through transferred shadows.'
All day the light bulb burns. A condemned cell?
And on the table, magazines, syringe,
flies suggestive of curdled food.
                            'Septicaemia,
and that umbrella raised by psychic force…'
Something must give. A growing urgency suggests
                          liquidation.
Nausea rises. Unable to find the door,
he regurgitates his nervous system
and shrinks as it tail-thrashes on the floor.

THROTTLING THE PILOT

Abrasive altitude fog-snakes Heathrow,
such scarlet runway-lights that define speed
are occluded, intermittent, then dead.
Klaxons patrol the vertigo
maelstromic in the cumulose sinews
of siamese-beige smog. The joystick threads
the turbines to their maximum circuit.
Nausea balloons its terminal green threat.

And one detached from his reservation,
operative on the transfusion of fear,
gun-walks his balance of a saboteur
in contracted bourbon-features.
An instant's annihilative future
determines his detonative façade;
green airline handbag armed with precision-
silencers. The turbines throttle back speed,

circumnavigating the control-tower.
Quavering in sense-querulous turmoil
the passengers vibrate in maroon-cells
paralysed by percussive height.
Hysterical to unseal a flight-door
through suicide victimise what's rational,
as height accelerates beyond the last
red signal, orbiting devoid of fuel.

from JUNKY TANGO OUTSIDE BOOT'S PICCADILLY

16
Someone was always standing in your head,
asking you to leave and with brevity.
You never knew his name. You came through
each time more damaged, more suspicious of
someone's recurring perfidy. An eye
polished with adrenaline: a body
in motion beyond blood's modulation.
Unable to desist. You lived on sky.

17
Was it at Teddington, your mainline fused? –
peristalsis and a white kindled blood
blasting the cosmic walls to Tarot cards,
each one a 12, you clinched into your clonic
respiration, pleading death rather than
an ambulance. You feared a hospital
more than a crab pincering its caged-pot.
We too, thought of the Lucozade-yellow

18
windows, remembered once at Hammersmith:
(your visit to the adjoining prison,
for one, inveterately incurable):
and how the windows weighed on tabid air
at four. Desultory as the draped bath-chairs
wheeled to the mortuary. We always are
by observation; but like a blind goat,
its eyes sewn up in the burial-pit

19
we panic, clutching at what passes through
and eaten by the necrogenes we burn
in lifting with hysteria. The telephone
shrilled constantly as we wound blankets round

your spasmic pumping. Days in bed, without
medication, while a brown-eyed night wind
felt in the ash tree for your body's parts:
waited for the distribution of bones.

20
And all the talismanic keepsakes of
your rooms, transposed from each to each in suit
cases; are now inventoried. Become
identiless ephemera, because
we are their meaning. And dead, constitute
the same vacancy as that surceased room,
that is a part of effete nonchalance.
A room in which the air becomes one's own:

21
something cognisant of intimate pain
at Chester Gate. Sir of the overdose-
goetia, you left your footprint on
the subway stair; I could not exorcise:
cut by the grief of a red winter dawn,
I went down on the Circle-Line's knocking
grids, so invested with amnesia –
I could not retain your mother's address:

22
still occupied with the putative; hoping
you would be at Catford; morose,
but still alive, resting with tenuity,
still able to see the gold carolus
beneath a dramatist's tongue. 17th & black.
The subway so abruptly inconsolable:
it too, a stasis of death's photograph
of cities; pariahs gone down to die.

CLAUSTROPHOBIA (KING'S CROSS)

I've gone down too often where
it's black and airtight, and I
can't stabilise, I lean against
the exit tunnel for what air
filters from the street at King's Cross,
uncertain whether to retrace
the means at moving back to light
on treads of the escalator.

I've suffered this to crisis-point,
the black sweat which is fear distilled,
and dread of consciousness lost to
the rush-hour pack. I've a card sealed
in my jumping fingers which reads
I am claustrophobic,
and gives my name and address but
I think of fainting as bloodshed,

of being mugged, my wallet and
pills gone, so too, secrets divulged
in that parting of the midriff
and head, that gap a divide
which won't heal back to consciousness.
I've lost my mind here and too far
to too many strangers, my need's
so strong it might involve the police.

And know at each renewal of
the maze, the dangers inherent
in potholing one's subconscious.
Keeping a whole city in poise
above, by balance of one's breath.
I lack this and emerge limpid,
trembling like a hare gone absent,
run through and out the ferret's teeth.

READING YOU RILKE

The house is silent. Reading you, Rilke,
I am invisible; my nerves attune
to a clairvoyant's over a crystal,
luminous in divination. It snows
inside the room, but outside it is clear.
I write my memoirs and remember you
first taught me how transitory are
perceptions and objects we thought most near.

I seldom range beyond this chateau's walls.
Without a mirror I'm two hemispheres
divided by an Alp. I disappear
into abstraction without poetry
as a source of outgoing. Two's too far
to offer comfort against space. It snows
inside the room, but outside it is clear.
I'll regain balance on some future star.

FACE TO THE WALL

January: the old no longer
retrieve mail from an unheated
hall. They tattle or whimper,

fearing geriatrics, forming
of the bedclothes a second skin,
afraid to augment the meter;

the room so dark it's like looking
through a head into depression.
Black lace antimacassars for

cheek-bones; the day at Notting Hill
herringed with frost, and who stirs
does so from tooth-ache or fingers

paretic with cold. There's no
protest, but a submissive will
to outlive those turned to the wall.

IN THE CHAIR

The portent's visualised and grows to be.
All afternoon the image of a man
bound to an overturned chair, invertedly
suspended from a motorway-bridge, turns
to redder sky, and in diminution

two men miniaturised on a ledge
observe this, receding into the black
shutter over the eye-piece of a
telescope; they altered perspective, so
now accelerate too fast to maintain
any semblance. – Flies passing through the eye

approximate. Analogous to how
the chair will later revert to upright.
He's where the men were and flying a kite.

METALLIC

Compelled disquietingly to focus
on things I can't assimilate, they are
all afternoon a mental irritant
I try to walk away from but walk with
and can't exorcise. They're mostly metal –
how observed discolourment blackly singed
the stationmaster's kettle seen at four
through the ticket grid. It seems to correlate
with how decades corrode and leave one dark
as a cricket ball skinned of red leather,
the mind's slowing until its kernel shuts.
And there are hints of fear from building sites,
cold bus handles, then ochre petrol tanks
observed across a low tide estuary,
how they arrive with the wince of fillings,
the dentist blind, and no anaesthetic.

A JUMP IN THE PICTURE
for John Robinson

It wasn't that. A jump in the picture,
say London seen from Muswell Hill, a red
sunlight framing the perspective after
thunder, the whole prospect unreal, the way
conceptual juxtaposition alters
on the canvas when the artist is dead,
and his original intent shows through
to who observe that superimposed light
which may not clarify for centuries
what had been a wrong way of seeing to
a composite design. It seemed like that,
this sudden dislocation, how I was
correcting this manuscript centuries on,
hoping that someone inadvertently
would open a book and observe the words
changing of their own accord, and how you
in whom my love had been unrequited
were sitting here, saying it's still hopeless,
rain falling on the inside of a window
without glass, and in your no fingers, a rose.

THREE DEVILS REEF

I heard him bunched down chattering
to the ebb-tide, on clinical parole.
The sea steaming West of Three Devils Reef –

a white alliterative damnation.
Both sea and sky suddenly moving left;
the right a black impenetrable wall

that follows his simian agility.
He keeps moving left, pursued like that
perverse estrangement that enrages bees

to misrender an attack on their queen,
and squall a face to a bubbling red pin-
cushion of strings. He runs ten yards, then drops

to wash his face in a rock-pool, resumes,
repeats; then prays with his mouth in water.
The pool ignites into stunning colour

over which wavers an indignant bee
transmitting attack-signals to the inshore
hive. Across the hinterland I hear

the cry of insane inmates, and white coats
that were running suspended in mid-stride:
(thirty held motionless while the landscape

does the running away). He keeps on left,
while the black swallows the coast as he tires.
The cliff I stand on narrows to a rope.

VISIT TO GEORGE BARKER

Under a chill sky of Northumbrian grey,
wind nettling the chinese-puzzle of lanes:
and at last to find intuitively your farm,
the headlights smoking while the dark closes
behind us to reveal a yard.
                                 Reclusive
but active, (so imagined of admired),
still advocating a dedication
resolute through so many years of trial.
Inspired now, by so desolate an Itteringham,
I understood the pony-post, sparse tiles,
your pilgrimage to Thurgarton.

An impenetrable blackness, guessed of green,
in tattersalls adjacent to your writing room,
seemed apposite with the cloud-mottled streams
enhancing your nervous cadence
of words subdued to lyric speech.
                                 Half stooped,
reflected red
by a log-fire, estranged by insecurity,
I wondered at your remote poverty;
the damaged books, incessant alcohol,
seclusion from the new adversary –
poets whose very aim is minimal
gesture, earning your dismissal.

And how this farm seemed your last hurt retreat
from denudation, penury, or worse
the climacteric impotence of words;
that age discounts sagacious voice
to a belittled impetus.
                         Children
keep ever-green
whatever arterial autumn awaits
in portent of fatigue. Beyond the gate,

the fields open to speculative black,
an inn crouched like a hedgehog on the track,
as talk distilled itself to ember, smoke
blue as the sky-race of Norfolk.

Itteringham: Norfolk

MARLOWE'S LETTER TO THOMAS WALSINGHAM

1   Unsearchably abject, burnt in death's groin,
    I write to you Thomas, from Temple Stairs;
                in trepidation
    of the dawn. Blood from Caesar's Tower oils
    the barking choughs, and a waterman snorts
    through mist.
                Genning's bloodily butchered stare
    still glowers, tigered with Gregory's succour;
    his severed tongue relinquished from his bowels.
                Abjuring Poley,
    exposes me to those complicities
    of State, as incise a fish-knife in the bladder.

2   Raleigh's at Sherborne; and Kyd at Bridewell,
    subjected to pincers. Who thrashed on straw
                    muddied by warders' boots
    would deny a psychopannychismic soul,
    and tongueless, foam before inquisitors?
    Red light
            clarifies the gobble of mud
    in recess with the tide; and a dog howls
    from London's pancreas. Of Scadbury
                    the trinkets of an
    escritoire, and heroic verse survives,
    small surrogates for a vacated skull.

3   Everywhere, the plague's black eczema boils
    rapaciously. Its poison-sack festers
                    on the river's tail,
    and Avernus gulps for Cynthia's heels.
    Her Tudor skin's become a stretched purple.
    Treason
            would make the old queen choke for blood.
    Greene's dead. His tapir-mouth's invective
    swallowed by his own obesely puce jowls

I think of Frizer:
an ear in abeyance to your shoulder;
his pronounced lip, obsequious in the corridor.

4   Cold light. Someone gargles in the river,
urinous with wine lees. The State's a skunk
                moistening its lair,
divaricating us who must hang limp
for other passions. I bite Charon's ears,
and stamp
                the myrtle into a red bruise.
Bruno's heart is an orange of blood-fire,
and proves like Dee, theosophy's gold ball
                an occultation
of the astrolabe. Why should not the moon
ignite our nerve like Christ's blood boiling in a bowl?

5   Certainly Frizer's pate tonsured with tar,
and cleavered in liberal hemispheres
                preoccupies my
mind with savagery. The Privy Council
appoints its simulatory stable-boys
better
                to instigate my apostasy;
and scald my scrotum on the torture-rack.
Pluto would wheeze his insatiable cluck
                of approbation
to perceive fundaments as mauve as plums,
flogged lame by the torturer's muscled back.

6   An aubade from Ovid suffices our
distempered crypticity. At Deptford,
                one Eleanor Bull's,
I meet Christ's octopus; tentacular
emissaries who would prefer a doll's
leather-
                muscle, to Phillip's genitals,
when the Queen beats like a black swan on Lethe,
and ceases pondering her strawberries.
                How long can Essex

prevaricate, one foot in the vortex?
The Spanish peacock moulting gold feathers.

7   Orange, rancorously redoubtable,
Whitgift stands as if embalmed in sulphur;
                his scarlet eyeballs
colloquising, as a sheep's uterus
bobs on the river. Spared the rack and wheel,
his teeth
        seem to solder a musket-ball,
and hiss for his concubine at Cherwell.
He thinks of Latimer, Ridley, Cranmer:
                black teeth crackling fire
before the rammed, intestinal poker.
Cerberus snuffles saffron saliva.

8   The city drums a scarlet dragon's pulse;
too many heads are spiked. Even our lice
                become pernicious
termagants, wriggling in State machinations.
The headless wives of Henry's atrophied
semen,
        still walk the river, vicious with
recrimination. Anne Boleyn's mauve lip
curls to imprecate: 'Henry, your bloated
                bull's neck sizzles
with syphilis, your libidinous rise
is short-lived, impotent as the Pope's nose.'

9   Our archives concealed in Durham House,
decoded, would mean impeachment without trial.
        Raleigh's careless of
spies. Perrot, Hariot, and Forman dare
the blue and lard-basting thongs of the fire
which chars
        propinquity to a red ash.
Neither Throckmorton's black pudendal rose,
nor Elizabeth curtained in Syon House,
        clinkers my vitals.

       Rather a youth's peach-taffeta shoulders
       shadowed above carp ageing in your pool.

10   The river calls. Where once its plangent swans
       fashioned their shadows on the current's drift,
                     its sagacious burn
       in hurdles. Alchemist, and theosophist
       are suspect, impugned under heresy.
       Acid
                 again explodes inside the wrist.
       I think across the irreparable gulf.
       Sweet-william, gillyflower and rose,
                     dazzle your estate;
       the more poignant for my portended threat.
       And you, Tom, have gone to the pool to fish.

LATE ONE
In memory of Albert Collier

Posthumously you'll have to read this one
who knew me; judiciously circumspect;
fifty years seniority when we met;
I solitary, reading Hart Crane in sea rain,

and you of the stammer, tutorial
with poetry, and reading my initial
scripts. Ostracised man of lonely rooms,
you parked your car adjacent to the sea,

routinal each day, contemplating white
Atlantic ledges, haggled with seabirds;
a foghorn plangently mewling address
of mist; then only the sleet of spindrift.

What you bequeathed was not eponymous.
It fulfilled my youthful vacuity,
those clandestine meetings; to friends you were
a life given as wholly personal.

No exactions, that rare empathy shared
by the incongruous of age. What was
intimated at was abjured against.
I still come to your parking spot, and surf

boils off the headland, turns an orange buoy
to a snorting hog. It's the sadness of
lights remembered coming on in hotels
overlooking the bay that defines grief.

You died unknown to me; a cardiac
seizure in a communal ward. I throw
a pebble down into the cliff hollow.
Its rattle seems your voice choking for words.

JOHN CLARE'S JOURNAL

Conjunctivital, lame, his nose dripping,
I teach a poor boy and refuse his coin,
and would rather have him read Thomson's *Spring*
than pore over figures scrawled on a slate.
Outside it rains, and my chrysanthemums,
claret, canary-yellow, white, agate,
show double flowers; and it rains
over Helpstone, and mires the country lanes.

For months, uncommonly depressed, I've sat
and watched the seasons fail, and felt a dark
oppress me, and I've stared out like a rat
from a wood-pile, terrified when I die
my sins will twist like ivy round a bark,
and leave me a lost wraith. Sometimes I cry,
and fear my family's ruin.
Everywhere the red crackle of autumn

lights brief fires; crimson hip, haw, glossy sloe,
hawthorn, and plum, black bryony berry
are winter portents, and my asters glow
in their pied embers. The same pious books
arrive from Radstock, and Taylor defers
my proofs away in London town. A rook
fares better on sparse carrion,
than I the proceeds of my rusty pen.

And still they linger, Billing's late swallows
fan the burgundy air of October
and with their late departure, I'd follow
into the blue sky, and be free. My themes
are no more fashionable than Bloomfield's were,
and he too, starved. Twice I've risen from dreams,
imagining my children laid
out as corpses by a potato spade.

And now that seasonal star, the Michaelmas
daisy, shows in blue clusters, and yellow
ruffles of chestnut leaves stipple the grass.
The little harvestbell quakes in the wind,
ragwort and marjoram linger below
the hedgerows, and twist thin threads, like my mind,
that's racked and vague. Sometimes I see
my own double madly pursuing me,

and then I cower for days in a wood,
or take to the road with gypsies, broken,
and better drunk. A poet's understood
a century too late; men badger words
into affected grace, an unspoken
eloquence, with grammar a two edged sword,
soon rusty, cast into a pool
where books are ballast for the ship of fools.

Twelve months to set a title page; small fame
for I who charm a lyric from the air,
and suffer quibbling editors who blame
me for my wrong spelling. In Lolham Lane
I found dwarf polypody, and read Blair,
and listened to the slow, fly-flashing rain
tinkle in the flood pits. Alone,
my mind becomes one with the grass and stone.

Better to be a botanist, and mark
each seasonal change, and what's peculiar
to one's native region. A huge crow carks
above me, and for three minutes I've timed
a snail's progress over a slender spar
of twig. Thirteen inches: a track aligned
without a shift to left or right:
such close-up conditions a poet's sight.

A coppled crowned crane shot at Billings pond,
a gypsy wedding over at Milton,
or a rare white maidenhair fern or frond

distracts me from the melancholy hours
I sit and ponder over Chatterton,
or muse upon the coloured plates of flowers
in Maddox's Directory –
the white peony and red anemone.

They say Byron uses a whip upon
whatever woman inspires him to verse,
and then hangs her up as a skeleton
for crows to peck. Humbled on a cart track,
my inspiration's more a wolf-eyed curse
that keeps me penniless, nosing the black
tunnels a mole snouts in my brain,
vacant for hours, and hatless in the rain.

I dreamt I died last night, or else I fled
into an unfamiliar country
enclosure had parcelled off, and instead
of finding refuge, I was hunted out,
and forced to stare into a bear's red eyes
and dance with it on a rail-line. A shout
started me, and a bailiff's grip
on my shoulder, worked up and split my lip.

I sit, tussled as my limp hollyhocks,
and watch a beggar pass. Driven from farms,
men scavenge aimlessly; the gypsies knock
and fiddle me a tune. Today I fear
a black shape that has spindle legs and arms,
and grows to envelop the sodden shire.
I am a wart between its eyes,
and yet I blow a grassblade while I cry.

DWIGHT'S BROTHER

From that platform, his aerial survey
monitors the world's missile-corridors,
the fretwork on the screen's like coloured dye
injected for the scan of an X-ray
highlighting the brain's arteries. The sky's
a bubble policed by piranha, and we,
slow fish in a pool, ghost our cooling star

towards its extinction. Dwight lives up there,
encased in glass, his ordnance of the blue
dependent on a hair-fine sanity
he vents on me, his paralysed brother,
who read all day in a bunker, and try
to calm him on his drunken visits here.
Sometimes, he says it's happened, and we're through

with breathing, and the stratosphere's alight
with marker flares. He cracks the star bourbon
we've cased in here, and wildly flaps a ball
across a pingpong table, half the night,
and then searches the reinforced white walls
for fissures. His nervous garrulity
leaves him supine, and scarlet eyed at dawn.

Sometimes I read his private dossier,
the lethal fall out of plutonium
from failed navigational satellites,
the leakage from nuclear storage pools,
the whole pejorative ballistics threat,
and worse, his manic hypochondria,
his gnawing fear of fatal infection,

his close studies of Manson and Nixon,
the monomania that burns planets.
Often, for weeks under security,
he undergoes strict immunisation,

his brain cells made into a ziggurat
of future galaxies. His marble skin
is aerosoled to a germless comfort.

Once, lying here inside an airtight calm,
my brother's chauffeur called, an ex-Nazi
who'd undergone a sex change; he'd survived
atomic research, and the East's braindrain
prior to Nuremberg, and stayed, and danced
before my spotlight. He supported arms,
but wore delicate colours round his eyes.

Each day the sky seems nearer: what Dwight fears
are stealth aircraft who bypass detection
in their inerrable vigil over
a planet they'll ignite. No survivor
will withstand the ozoneless atmosphere,
except in these villages of bunkers
built mole-like in the earth's rotating cone.

Sometimes it catches me out: the sure hum
of the earth's spinning, and I lose control,
imagining the encompassing void,
and the red of a post-nuclear sun;
and built beneath the camp's, the tunnel road
I explore in my invalid's car when
Dwight's done, researching reactor-vessels,

preparing for a conference. Today
I drove on in too far: the lights shut out,
and my engine went dead, while I could hear
someone running towards me, then away,
or was it the trick of a generator?
Madness, I thought, 's like a kitten at play,
it unravels the mind, until we shout,

or lose identity. And then I saw
them, huddled in a group, three who had cracked,
and taken refuge here, and claimed they were

survivors of the universal flaw.
They carried me captive through a trapdoor
to a cellar of scavengings, offal,
and on their screen the first missile attacked.

CARTFORD

Perhaps it took minutes to register;
he daydreaming of an amanuensis
his impoverished stipend
wouldn't cater for; and he the vicar
of a wayward parish, and a bachelor
sipping sherry over a bland sermon,
he'd blotted, in the quiet of his study,
a late bee, busy at the snapdragons

in the chalk blue of the June afternoon,
while he recollected Brooke's Grantchester,
and squinted into a sunbeam
preferring to remove himself in time,
then leaving his eye search among the lime-
tree, for the song of a linnet. Perhaps
this man of the sable cloth was so far
away, dreaming of places on the map

of his native Dorset, he never heard
the abrupt expiry of an engine
overhead in the cloudless blue;
but went on listening to that jovial bird,
while a red monoplane catapulted
to wreckage, and exploded in a wood,
so that dry foliage burst into flame.
If he heard it, he never understood

its import, but mused on the green quiet
of the old walled garden. His parish seemed
docile as a centuries' old moat
in which the elder flowers were afloat
in a liquid reflection; the hamlet
as yet unthreatened by bellipotent
marauders. If he dreamed, he was startled
by distant shouts, and wondered why they lent

no urgency to his unruffled mood,
and thought it part of a dark reverie
about the cross, he'd not resolved;
and paced the garden, as one might who dreads
the advent of a terrible threshold,
and leaves that night for a distant country.
He must have left without closing the door,
and run out with his face turned to the sky:

certain it was, he never once looked back,
or was sighted. We took the remains there,
expecting his full blown cassock
to offer comfort, and bless the pieces;
the doctor distant on his country round.
Perhaps we didn't comprehend, nor he
the oddity of worse than death, who ran
away but not from our calamity.

ADAM

It wasn't old age or incontinence,
the absent-mindedness to match two shoes,
or walking around unzipped worried us,
you largely housebound, but a reversion
to primordial instincts, how each day
we'd find you digging the earth with your hands
at the garden end, scooping one neat hole,
and obsessively digging until noon
made you uneasy, and you'd guard your trench,
one ear pressed to the earth as though alert
for a first seismic tremor then a split
dividing the planet in one neat line.
In time we came to forget who you were.
A father, grandfather, great grandfather,
and noticed black hair covering your skin,
coarse and hirsute as an ape, and left you
beating your tail out in the night garden,
the whole gradually unearthed, you slept out,
reading the book, shouting your name, Adam.

ON ARRIVAL

They'd dropped the coffin with a marker-flare
vertically from two thousand feet into
a trench inlined with Bacon anamorphs

and blow-ups of forensic photographs;
the aim precise; the casket unsplintered.
We raced to intercept it in our car,

following trails of coloured vapour left
by a low aeronautical display.
We'd waited days for this red semaphore.

And drove with headlights on against a sun
which seemed to quiver like a detached eye
fastened to a tenuous optic nerve.

And as we drove, the sky seemed circular,
a stereo record played in reverse.
Its grooves were mauve and white cleats of vinyl.

And you were anxious with your camera,
looking for findings at the speed of light,
and curious about this funeral,

how we were suddenly in contact
with a cancer-conference, police radar;
suicides eating after autopsies.

And arrived to find the coffin aglow.
Your camera flashlight detonated on
impact. The jets were falling with red snow.

SWEET JAR

I entered quietly and heard the needle
vibrate in your arm from a passing train.
You'd stood it wrongly and punctured a vein,
and blood was profuse; it covered your arm.
I'd come with gelignite in a sweet-jar
to satisfy your clandestine uses.
You had a means of psychic infiltration,
of tweezering it into other minds,
and then detonating it by staring
so fixedly the victim's circulation
ceased. His packed skull would blow through the ceiling.
You'd never speak. I stood there with a towel,
and you, misinterpreting this, motioned
upstairs to a bath containing a skull
on a plug-chain. You'd use lipstick on it,
designating areas of attack
for future victims. (Each was an experiment,
not a murder.) For days prior to each
killing, your adrenaline would be like jet-fuel.
It had to issue through another's head
in order to be pacified. This time
you were going to tell me how many
grains you'd infused into my blood-pressure,
how long before your duplicity would kill.
I stood holding a torch and watched you bleed.
You wanted the sweet-jar placed in the fire.

PARALLEL ORANGE

You peel an orange on the counterpane.
I'm miles away but olfaction intrudes
to the nether lip. Here the road divides

into a complex interchange, gradients
calibrated by tyre-pressure; to skid
would leave a driver fossilised outside

the crash, hung up like a spider's trophy
hundreds of feet above the burning car.
I never did believe in hitch-hikers

as palpable, they're who behind barriers
keep signalling, unaware that they're dead.
Each car is photographed and towed away;

the doctor fixing a morphine syringe
into the driver's seat, simulating
the fatality as a red blanket.

The victim watches it, inexorably
cut off. An orange was in a dashboard-
compartment. Miles away you bite the skin.

BY THE FISHERIES

The sea's translucent here, slowed to a calm
by an opposing breakwater, a form
of improvised harbour – its concrete arm

projected to oppose a running grey
current that's never still, but turns over
the way a leaf might, caught up in the spray

of a waterfall to expose markings
of jasper and lime as an underside
to galled blues, here contained as in a ring

siphoned off the channel by industry.
Here where a desalination plant churns
its outwash into a let of the sea,

and the zinc buildings of a fisheries
are cantoned above a hollow backdrop,
I stand, fishing that pooled serenity

for mullet, and watch sunlight make a star
on the shards of a broken gin bottle.
The aim's to cast wherever shadows are

composed by cloud, and not the diffusion
of one's image breaking up in water.
I watch my float's spherical orange cone

calligraphise its motion on the glare
that strikes the water like molten lead poured
into a sheet that furnaces on air,

and hangs there in a cobalt flame. A man
trundles an offal barrow to a bin,
and stands a long time with a yellow can,

staring at my immobile silhouette,
pensively tilted back into shadow,
my features guarded by a wide-brimmed hat,

and then deposits what looks like the flash
of a signet ring into the water –
his hollow beer-can lands without a splash.

I don't look up, rather I watch the shoal
jolt with that vibration, and jump like nerves
startling their own reflections back to real.

COMPOSITION

His red silk necktie flares, and moodily
she's turned to watch a tufted duck's apache

black head streak rival the mallard's turban
of iridescent silks, and shelducks scan

the sky's cameo in the lake. The lime
tree smells of rain – a scent come from the shine

of an old pocket in which coins have lain.
The jasmine's musty, and azaleas stain

the water madder rose. It's sharper now
the shower's build-up, and a greylag scows

for shelter. Why it is that two conflict
upon a scale of moods he can't predict

a pattern to's the puzzle, like this lake's
alphabet of V's – web-footed duck wakes

that cut the green silk to a convict's cloth
of arrows. A swan turntables a wreath

on the darkening water, and he draws
his mind back in, edging for words to thaw

a silence, cold as a quartz vein in stone,
and then she's plunging, as her opaline

necklace splits on its string – each green bead's lit
by a raindrop scoring a perfect hit.

CHRISTOPHER SMART IN MADNESS

They spare me Bedlam for St Luke's Shoreditch,
who am appointed heir to King David,
and fester here where rabid
cries accompany Battie's enquiry
as to madness, whence comes this divine itch
to see into the limits of the sky?
I trundle God's gold ball in Satan's ditch.

They bait me like a bear. My creditors
are importuning demons who'd usurp
my episcopal claims. They hurt
my fevered head, and festinate the ague,
so that I shrink back in my noisome lair,
and crouch there, distracted, unwitting, vague.
The fire of ADORATION burns my hair.

My wife's a Moabite, a Newbery
for whom I squandered my pen in burlesque
before the angelic lyre struck
my holiness to David. Now I pray
that all hurt things are of one ministry.
Listen, the redbreast sings in February,
appointed angel to our misery.

And I am delivered from London's news,
its pettifogging brawls. Johnson alone
gives meat to a dead skeleton
of words; and came by. How his linen stank,
like mine. His strength prevents him breaking
through to the other side of reason. I drank,
before a red cloud opened in the blue,

and I prayed vociferously to God,
and bound myself to the purgative wheel
which burnt the lining of my soul.
Jubilate Agno, they'd confiscate,

except my mind's like a worm in a clod,
which cut in half can still compose, secrete,
and render consecration to David.

Cuckolded, cheated of inheritance,
I shiver here, and hear the sudden bell
of Staindrop Church. Lilac umbels
chequered the grass, the wild polyanthus,
I picked for one Anne Hope, and then in trance,
saw our heavenly marriage through stained glass.
God's voice was further then. I had distance.

And now a pauper go. My alms are words
of prophecy. God lit my candlestick's
orange and immutable wick,
but still they never see. Harping-irons
prod us to tasks, who cower here in dread,
and see rats catch the bread for which we pine,
and hungry, live upon raw gin instead.

Let Peter rejoice with the white moon fish
that's radiant in the dark, and let attend
Jesus on us, unsound of mind,
who cured Legion. My brethren here despair
of light, and must in other madhouses
repine for day; and go without repair.
I pray so loudly that the others curse.

The prison dampness comes to coat my skin
who venture in God's fire, and see the stone
on the right hand side of his throne
withheld from man. And gold within the dark,
I see the mine of Hell where the napkin
of the escaped Jesus still redly marks
the stone, and brooding on it I see Cain.

Outside it rains. I hear a horse collapse,
and men beat it ferociously with sticks.
It died. I pray God for redress

of all animal injuries. Tonight
I wept, and thought to incur a relapse,
and in his knowledge God brightened his light.
Tonight Christ's lantern swings inside this house.

HOUSMAN IN OLD AGE

The water's cold not tepid: an austere
face inquisitively feels the razor's
smooth passage induce no sudden bristle
or discomfort. (Once your criterion
for the awesome chill
attendant on a poem's inception.)
A long dormancy's blunted your response,
and if the razor slips, it's clumsiness,
not the sudden impulse of a lyric.
You've mellowed to a specious scholasticism,
and a bachelor's eccentric Cambridge walks.
Such is the age of one who wrote of youth.
The wasted years bay you like a gaunt wolf.

RIFTS
in memory of Eugenio Montale

The ivy leaf's a diamond-lit frog's back
after the sudden impingement of rain,
and drops ricochet from the waxing black

of the sloe-berry, and the queen of hearts
is multiplied on each fallen pear leaf.
If a bird drops down it's quick to depart,

its eye flashing faster than a raindrop,
and coloured with the premonitory South.
The woodlouse locks fast in the log's slow rot.

Alive, you followed rifts, a kingfisher's
brilliant flare igniting the slow pool,
then imperceptibly lost in azure,

or the smoke spiral of a ship's funnel
hanging in a slow S while mist dispersed
to a rainbow. On cobbled flats runnels

tingled with light – each sea-pool a mirror
pointing you to the still more vibrant stars,
and sitting late the porcupine's tremor

was the first hint of storm, as a fish net
lifted by the gust concurred with lightning.
All life's the startled bolt of a mullet

disturbed by a shadow and gone so quick
we think it forever in migration.
You watched for breaks and knew the erratic

wavering of the sea-bound butterfly
touched on the very pulse of light, and drew
from its frenetic course a harmony

all light-borne creatures have. Word after word
catches fire in your work as mist singes,
and through its red hoop darts the migrant bird.

VISITING HOURS

I try to reach you who reverse in years
to a child lost inside a labyrinth,
and it seems you're my son now, not father,
and it is I who must answer questions
by a frightened bedside, and allay fears
that root in you, and by circumvention
of facts, pretend that it's an interval

of rest you're here for, not a terminal
illness; and that this bed, this window pane
dustily framing the roofs of London
is the last corner that that you'll come to know
on earth; the ward for four, circumspect walls
of white, the soundless television screen
that's on all day, and the routinal pills

that deaden your cancer's anabasis,
steroids to reduce brain inflammation.
Fifty-eight years without a day's illness,
and now your helplessness is of a child's
fumbling for speech, for a balance that's gone,
and leaves you without co-ordination,
seeking sleep, like a diver gone on down

to find an exit that was always there,
but never used. Each day you go deeper
in that exploration, while we in air
can only call you from a great distance,
and meet you when you surface. Who's farther
from whom? I only know you need me here,
as once you comforted me in nightmare.

You hold my hand as though I were a spool
playing you out lifeline with each visit,
hoping that thread's unbreakable. Your pull
is vibrant at all hours, and the welts cut

each time you awake to panic or fear,
and I can sense your knowledge that you are
a hooked salmon who can't jump from the pool.

The prospect narrows. Standing in the sun,
I see my own death frozen in a beam,
as it will isolate me years later,
and I without offspring. You are my son
in these last weeks. A huge jet lifts over
the city; then the ward reverts to calm.
I too fear the end of visiting hours.

LUMBER ROOM

The dark inside smelt of convolvulus
gone musty after rain, and a pappus

of dust thistled each cobweb's tarnished watch–
interior. Light let in by the latch

was a diamond ray tapped out to a code –
a migraine to the spider's eyes to goad

it out of its Lilliputian parasol.
Inside, I listened to the martial roll

of small disturbances, and a soot–fall
of air moved with me. It was ritual

this going back upon a scent to find
a burial enacted in the mind –

a child standing before a cracked mirror,
its irezumi mask of bright colours

a solitary Noh drama, while the rain
was a horse's tail swishing flies, a stain

that mouldered in the rafters. Turpentine,
old jaundiced books, tied up trunks, and a wine-

bottle with stalactites of wax were my
discoveries, familiar genies

for a child's magic, listening to his thoughts
name symbols for their colours, while the knot

of the bunched spider stirred like breaking ice
inside the thumb-screw pincers of a vice.

CONGER

A conger's world is tubular, it means
seeing things thinly through a gun-barrel
from the point of view of the bullet-head
that's primed to fire, the fist-sized, clam-tight jaws

more deadly in their lock than a bulldog's.
They'll shave a finger off with precision,
clean as a horse bite, or close round a hand
and leave it as taut gristle strung on bone.

The colour of beached wrack, or an old tom
that's greying, these inhabit wrecks, or lairs
from which their protruding head is streamlined
like a grounded jet's. Fastened to a spar

they'll fight on a short fuse, and savagely
bite free of suction pads working to grip
the powerful torsion of the body's girth.
In biting, their mouth opens from a slit

to an alsatian's wide full-toothed gullet.
Conger stay low, anchored to the sea-bed,
solitary killers holed up in their dens,
they mostly go unchallenged, like this head

which would swallow a sewer-rat or cat
washed out to sea; engorge it, and lie low
until nightfall, and then seek out new prey,
killing with a psychopath's will to slow

the moment to all time. Dragged to the air,
a conger barks, and if not killed outright
will live a day, and still retaliate.
This black boothead dazzled by a boat-light,

come loose of the hook, might jump at a throat,
and drag a man down, who stands shrinking back,
petrified at this one to one combat;
a jerky lighthouse twitching through the black.

AIR

Rain water brushed from a swift's pointed wings
on to an eyelash or a spider's web
is how I like to think of the exchange

of altitudes, a vibrant resonance
on this gusty day with birds ticking South
through a needle's eye, each propelled in trance

to dare luminous wind-shafts, and one feels
the elasticity of their wing-pull
in the air's simmer – the twitch of their pole

asserting gravity. The earth transfers
their arrowed passing as the aftermath
of hooves. I crouch down low and consider

the one vertical between me and space
that's flying westwards with the Atlantic,
and watch a singular whitewashed lighthouse

bulb on its rock. Out here the pulse of air
tingles with light hexagonals, I see
it transformed into design and colour

such as the intricacies a snowflake
contrives in fashioning its slow descent.
I sense those sharp intangible facets

pass through me, diamonding the light the way
hail flashes on a heated shovel's back,
or a cormorant's sheen glistens with spray

that smokes on its alighting. Sea and sky
in one illimitable rush of blue
open up light worlds, and the tern's shrill cry

untranslatable holds me static here,
given over to such fluidity
I am become a component of air.

STICK BY STICK

A stoked temper's a big cat in the blood,
and flickers of heat lightning tell me that
the imminence of your unleashed outrage
will suddenly strike like a ball a bat

sends crashing to the boundary. All day
the air's been touchy as a nettle patch,
and breathing in the sultry heat I smell
the crackle of a gorse fire a flipped match

sets blazing in crisp furze. If there's a leak
it taps like an oil drip on a wet road,
a blood-count spiralling to combustion,
so that the red fleck in your eyes explodes

to the wild bloodshot of an outpaced horse.
The room contracts, and its rice-paper walls
threaten to let the neighbours in; I hear
your fist beat a hornet's nest to a squall,

each irascible word, armed with a sting
that goes so deep, I come to doubt that we
are human in this combat, locking skulls,
squid-eyed, reduced to a monstrosity

we doubt as real, but think we act the parts
in a blood-letting; a wolf spider's itch
to entice the male to white sexual heat,
then pick its eyes out in a bone-dry ditch

before the rain storm floats both on the froth
of its torrential stream. We gag for air,
clumsy as seals, wading in divers' boots,
cumbersome, frazzled by the lightning's glare,

two wasps simmering over shattered jars
of jam, a broken chair, smashed tabletop,
licking our sores amongst that jellied flow,
too tired to go on, and too mad to stop.

DEAD HAND

His dead hand catches, while the right secures
clothes randomly discarded on a bed,
garments he's seen worn once or twice before,
but kept in store, that velvet suit and red

silk shirt, the water reflections of ties
contrasting lapis lazuli with grey
shot silk – vestiges of a taste that lacked
courage to wear them, now exposed today

on counterpane and floor, a mosaic
to be boxed up and sent to charity
bazaars. His right hand's an inert puppet
that needs constant attention as though he

composed all movement to accommodate
its handicap, nursing it to repose
on safe surfaces. Cautiously he swabs
a thin red line issuing from his nose,

and addresses the empty room, while cold
sunlight whitens the pane, and forms a star
diffusing itself in oblique sunbeams.
He thinks, how in seconds he's come so far

towards the edge of being, that he knows
all time encapsulated in one stare,
and composed of his loss. His dead hand drags,
as on one knee he faces the harsh glare

of sunlight, and tucked beneath his good arm
a bourbon bottle's cradled. Down below,
the reverberation of stalled traffic
makes him conscious of the open window,

he slumps by, quickened by the frosted air,
and looks across at a removal van,
and concentrates on its blanketed wares,
his dead hand gummed to an open paint can.

THE STORM

A wasp's vibration in a gorse-flower,
that orange flame belling the wings' motion,
was how it seemed miles distant, the tremor

of a needlehead dropped from a great height
into the uncorked bottleneck we cooled
in a sea-pool. All afternoon the light

blazed iridescently ultramarine
on a sea surface fixed like an eye-glass
into the peacock of the horizon;

the hours afloat, and a torpid sea-bell,
leisurely tinkling; and you with a pen
and red ink, fashioned a memorial

to the dead seagull found upon the cliff
in our descent. A gruff buzz of black flies
sounded like a kitten's purr on the path

as they stippled that carrion. And down
below, the calm was eerie, and the lull
seemed like the sky and sea stood still, one calm

reflection, lacquered over with gold flecks
in lapis lazuli. We trod water,
or lay immobilely upon our backs

cushioned by the salt bay; and then it grew
this hairline of cobalt, to a fissure
of massing cloud, an ink-dot in the blue

expanding to a welled concentration
of angry mauves, and marbled quartz, and red,
and we could hear the thunder's vibration

stalk like a big cat growing voluble
behind the incandescence of its cage.
Then rain, each drop shiningly audible,

clopping into the sea, and shimmering
with a dragonfly's bright translucency,
each globule expanding to a white ring.

We took refuge before the downpour steamed
cleansingly through crevice and flaw, and smoked
skywards. You drew the lightning flares as red

unskewered spiral hairpins jumpingly
illuminating a cobalt skydrop,
while I saw the future, a butterfly

escaping its chrysalis, and on stone,
resting a while, before the longer flight,
sure like the migrant swallow of its home.

SPIDER FIRE

The popping crackle of dry sticks, the hiss
of catching gorse and broom, had routed out
all small things from the undergrowth, fieldmouse
and shrew, the glinting tick of the grass-snake,
squirrel and weasel, touchpaper-rabbits,
the conflagration spreading, red and blue
quiverings of flame quick to overtake
the fire's orange centre, timothy grass
and thistle sucked into the twitching crack
of the irregularly sheeting wave,
birds had gone in advance of the smoke plume,
rooks heckling in their flapping sky traffic,
chased off by a shuffling necklace of stones,
marigold, scarlet, crazy yellow whirrs
jumping a cow-gate, scorching the farm track . . .

What was the fire's shock through a spider's eyes?
The agelena's horizontal web,
pegged to a blackthorn hedge, scintillating
with rainbow filaments, male and female
telephonic in their alarm signals,
the vibrant nerves unleashed from a tight ball,
acrobats dropped down to the maze-forest
of verticals, a field away the roar
gaining in volume, everywhere a migratory
diaspora of insects, tunnelling,
feeling forward with bristling antennae,
the tenacious marauding wolf-spider
running across hairline fissures, halting
like someone pulled up short by a mirror;
some missing legs, armour-plate or an eye,
embattled hunters chased out of the field
by a seismic explosion, shivering
in the long drag of smoke, their collective
panic inducing a telepathy,
a radar bleep signalling the way out.

I watched from the hill's summit; a black hoop
ironed into the shire was a ring of ash
incinerating insects in its char.
The farm was black struts, ember-glowing spars.
Some must have made it to the other side,
two spiders having crossed a continent,
digging in, letting the earth still, aware
they'd made it, smoke-blind, too tired to hide.

DEAD WEASELS

I found them hanging, strung up on grey cord,
five of them, gagged together with jackdaws,
the branch weighted like a poulterer's hook
with carrion worn through to their skeletons,
the walnut-sized ivory skull of a rook
had come loose of its rain-moulded bark-stiff
feathers, flushed on dead leaves no fox would sniff.
Dead silence, the wood stark, old beech, old elms,
defiantly rooted against the cold,
and, at the field's edge, rabbit diggings, flint
thrown up on the furrow. The light was gold
on plum-stained brambles. Somewhere else a gun
was barking sporadically at pheasants.
I swung the weasels round to catch the sun,
their long, slender bodies hung vertical,
the fur a straggling ripple on the bone
was like a current chased out in a stream,
the forepaws stylised, were two brittle hands
raised in supplication. The vice-locked head
seemed more a conger's raised to fight the gaff,
the jaws open upon their needle teeth
as though frozen in the bloody second
of ripping into a mole or chicken,
fast night-hunters who companion the owl's
plummet at a leaf-tick. These had their skulls
protruding through an envelope of fur,
crisp to a dryness that the thumb could peel,
rain-beaten fossils gone to matted rope
stringily twined, they looked like effigies
of a demonic rite without the pins.
I cut two down and placed them in a sack,
victims who'd raked the copse for pheasants' eggs,
and sucked them dry. They still had fine whiskers,
minute spiders bunched in the eye sockets.
Their combined weight was less than a finger,
their volatility still composite

in their death agony. Rooks and ravens
were thronging back in droves. I came on out
and crossed the field, my presence scaring off
two short-fused rabbits bolting for their dens.

WINTER MULLET

The sun's berry-red in a ruck of blue;
somewhere, recalling Webster, a robin's
melancholy song is premonitory
of blade-edged ice, frost engraining its pins

into a field corrugated by cold,
the furrow-mounts crisp as a sheet of glass.
I make my way towards a coastal drop,
the water there's nursed by a powerhouse,

a tepid current that attracts offshoots
from the densely packed, spawning winter shoals,
wedged tight like overlapping slates, silver
of a flick-knife's punched out when a fish rolls.

These are the winter mullet, somnolent,
their world shrunk to the dimensions of trance,
they are unfeeling, semi-comatose,
their vision almost dead, their slow advance

that of someone flexing inside a dream
they can't connect with. I flick a flyspoon
tipped with white ragworm out towards the shoal,
and have it flutter, a jittery moon

working the shallows like a butterfly,
invites no quick uptake. Amnesiacs,
they're living with dulled instincts, one ungroups
and eyes the spoon, but hangs there, changing tack,

his metabolic rate too slow to chase.
Two or three basking in the warm stream shift
my bait, boxers prodding at a dummy,
they lip it back and forth, hoping to lift

the worm's flicker from the barb that they've sensed.
They disengage, their curiosity's
soon extinguished. In summer, they're playful,
dribbling a dough-ball round a float, or free

to shoot ten yards at a compulsive flash.
I stay on, the cold chaps my fingers red,
its pimpling's like dried beads of black hemlock,
the fish have tightened now into a head,

a mint destined to fall foul of seine nets.
Men keep a watch on these. A figure throws
a light over me in the early dark.
I jump to meet it, moth-dazed by the glow.

ANTS

Ground-level scrutiny's what each convoy
        is versed in; on the march they are
like booted soldiers hand-picked to deploy

a valley-floor, their mandibles' fork-lifts
        manœuvering the incessant
lava of boulders and felled trees that drifts

across their path. They map a region by
        their purposeful dexterity,
so low down that they never know the sky's

more than a puddled mirror they look in.
        Vehicular, quarrying loads,
their chain-gang tenacity is a thin

red fuse that flickers like a second-hand
        wavering between numerals.
They're earthquake victims dusted by white sand,

jockeying baggage from the seismic flaws
        of a city gone underground,
firemen able to ascend vertical

faces with a stunt-car's lurching motion.
        They simmer noiselessly across
a cragged flagstone in tank-drill or cushion

a dead beetle on a mobile rickshaw,
        their bodies square like elephants
beneath the victim's weight. Fast, quizzical,

their reconnaissance combs a territory
        and strips it of each utensil
serviceable to their massed colony,

autocrats of a starved third world. Close up
        their eyes are headlights, the thorax
wing-polished by a chauffeur, their stirrup-

roll affords high suspension. Grave-robbers,
        they swarm to an uncapped jam-jar,
and sugar-drunk, mark time in the larder.

THE WAKE'S DEPARTURE

They're going home: headlights flare gold across
a farmyard, startling a grey nuzzling rat
into a straw pile; some have edged the weight
of a coffin's underside on shoulders
of suits so rarely aired they hold their crease
like a cricketer's whites. Lit by toddies,
even the moribund are jocular;
the body consigned squarely to its ditch,
the talismans divided, the estate
a widow's roof-leaking thatched usufruct.
They've placed his Sunday hat upon the gate.

BAUDELAIRE IN MIDDLE AGE

Fear is a parasite whose increments
expand to a void both inside and out,
we wear its countenance like the red cross
slashed on a blighted elm crippled by drought,

and yet we're dropsical, a polyp sack
weighs like a bladder at our arid core,
its pustules file into our blood, we choke
beneath the heavy swipe of Charon's oar

and raise a blue face to the waterline.
It's glacial despite the stifling heat
that grizzles Paris to a carpenter's
pepper of sawdust. Couples in the street

sense how I peel the foreskin from their skulls
with the dexterity of a fish knife
handled by a mortician – a draughtsman's
clean edge autopsying husband and wife

on their restless stomp up La Rue Cadet
to the Casino. My frosted white hair
and holed suit pinched upon the skeleton,
my eyeballs, blown up to a lobster's stare

before the boiling cauldron fires it red,
attract averted eyes. I hear them speak
of me as a defrocked priest, a debauched
scatologist whose skin smells like a leek,

and who goes hand in pocket to Ancelle
to keep his blowfly creditors at bay.
Age is a birthmark branded by a snake's
whiplash, a pip that ripens to decay,

not with the measured metronomic tick
of the clockhand on the Chambre Correctionelle's
pea-green wall where they ridiculed my book,
but with the electric jab of a bell

warning Nero Rome and his hair's on fire;
even one's lice atrophy and shrivel
to victims of vesicular famine,
a kind of green ooze mingles with one's smell,

and work, that groove in which we place our hand,
as in a vice, and tighten the thumbscrew,
becomes evasive, it slips like a fish
through eddies, leaving me to count the blue

moons scored upon my blotter, while the stair
creaks with some creditor's thug changing foot
with pins and needles. What can they salvage? –
no grave-robber's toothpick would find a boot

worth heeling, or a saleable work-sheet.
They sell *Les Fleurs du Mal* in the junk heaps
along the quays, its parchment paper soiled
by smutty fingers. No jackal on heat

would find kindling-sticks in the jewel-cold blaze
that packs each sensuous image with snow.
Brushed by the wing of madness, I shiver
above a spiral shaft of vertigo –

the city's tiny, it's a matchstick maze,
its citizens are chain-ants thrumming by,
each with a mule-eyed passiveness. They slow,
and drowsing I can hear the wheedling cry

of a starved cat kneading today's letter
from *Le Figaro* declining my work.
I stand up dizzy like a man lifted
off his feet by the hangman's sudden jerk.

HEIRLOOM

Your mouse-grey 1950s obstinate
Morris Minor, would wait upon the hill,
a battered perennial amphibian,
sheeted on coastal roads, driven until

its wear seemed contemporaneous with yours,
its interior smelt of wintergreen–
embrocation, it was your reading-room,
a snail's house slanted on a height between

two oaks and a mushroom-domed mulberry.
The sea beneath was like the turquoise eye
in a peacock's feather, or wintry grey,
slammed in the hollows, while an opaque sky

had lights come on like small aquarium fish
flickering in shoals round the coast. You read
for hours there, the thrillers of your youth,
the writers still alive, their novels dead.

That car bequeathed you by a friend was your
most intimate possession. Its headlights
were an ophthalmic frog's eyes, and its brakes
defied all but a tightrope walker's slight

response of pressure; you were the master
of an eccentric mechanism none
dared disattune. Often I'd trace your car
come out of a tunnel into the sun,

late autumn sunlight, and tick round the coast,
labouring the hill to this sheltered eyrie,
where gulls hung still, then lurched at a tangent
over some object imperceptibly

thrown up by the wave. Now that car is mine,
garaged after your death, its engine mute.
I walk back to your parking-spot, the waves
climb the rock-face and vertically salute.

REGULAR

One of a kind who finds sanctuary here,
withdrawn, pacing your drinks, circumspectly
dressed in a graphite pinstripe, your black eyes
sunk like a hamster's were an inventory

of small particulars, a pub's archives
impressed upon your mind's engraving-plate,
so many years spent watching on a stool. . .
Aloof, unfamiliar, you'd hesitate

over your choice of drink rather than have
the barman come to know your preference
between Johnnie Walker and Haig. You held
the liquid in your glass with deference

for its gold–spot of volatility,
and added water as though refilling
a deoxygenated goldfish-globe.
The admixture clouded, a tarnished ring

gone copper from the march of verdigris;
and if the liquor's burning took you where
you saw things double or in a vortex,
you remained dispassionate, a fixed stare,

inscrutable, conceding no gesture
of approbation or contempt. No one
intruded on the stool you'd ironed out.
You faced the bar like someone who has won

the right to be recognised, but ignored,
an oxygen plant drinking all the air,
so that the others laboured breathlessly,
contracting in a ring. Grease on your hair,

bootblacked its natural grey. You were a dog
begging acceptance, swallowing your bark,
following an invisible keeper
out of the swing-doors into the pitch dark.

NERO

It is so terrible a thing to die? –
Exile's a termite to the intellect,
one's lines resound against an empty sky
on some craggy outpost where goats dissect
a clifftop for a mouthful. None are spared,
even the household gods have rubbled heads,
the shrine of Vesta's defiled, and thunder
rumbles its omens over every bed.
Two-headed offspring, lightning bolts, a snake
a woman gave birth to, still dribbling red,
its markings interfaced with jewels, predict
the impending whirlwind we live under,
scattering Rome's twenty-one district plots
into a smashed mosaic, in its wake
a cone of fire spins to avenge this spot.

Matricide stains his bad blood with worse blood.
Agrippina, who curled upon her couch
enticing him to take her in a flood
of youthful frenzy, only had him touch
her pythonic hips through diaphanous
veils exposing her naked to her son.
He had her butchered, Britannicus too,
last of the Claudians, a brother done
to death, his gizzards shrivelled up in flame,
the whole deranged, effete imperial zoo
looking on, Burrus with his crippled hand,
Paris squawking, the eunuch retinue;
they buried him that night, even his name
was omitted from the ribald statue.

Men fear the streets at night, the drum-skin throb
of Nero's bacchanalia. He ties
his victims up in bearskins, and the mob
assaults them, gobbing spit into their eyes.
Poppaea rules his couch but cannot stem
a lust for every perversion; he rules

by virtue of Seneca's diligence,
a man whose austere philosophic school
accrues to it more riches than the state.
I envy Sullius his penitence
and soft Balearic exile; no poet
can publish, the Emperor has preference
over Lucan, my pine-enclaved estate
is eaten up by his indifference.

Our Empire cracks like worn crocodile skin,
it is a fishnet full of holes that flaps
at frontiers; Gauls, Frisians and Parthians
slough through the army's unprotected gaps.
Only in Britain does the eagle fly,
Suetonius licked a wild barbaric ruck
of troops marshalled by women – not a head
was saved – thousands stared from the horse-churned muck,
the smoking welter of a lashed rabble,
Boudicca's skin booted the blue of lead,
and yet that country's an untamed thicket,
its forests resist our tapemeasure roads.
Today our drill's the anaemic babble
of men who sit squat as paunch-bellied toads.

The model ivory chariots on his board
are playthings like the laurel that he wears
to face his golden statue with its bored
expression. Twenty times his height, it stares
towards the ceiling's fretted ivory.
The tyrant in the Golden House who sweats
beneath the lead weights placed upon his chest
for better respiration to abet
his vocal cords. His husky voice can't range
to the empyrean and when he rests
he wears a robe embroidered with gold stars.
Rome's become an international exchange
for gladiators, charioteers, mock wars,
there's not a statue's head that doesn't change.

His eye's his mirror, not a mirror stares
from the imperial rooms, in case she shows,
the dead mother who drags him by the hair
from sleep and suffocates him by a slow
immersion in an ant-hill. Nothing quells
the raging insomnia that has him run
tilting at statues, the amphitryon
of ransacked Greek gods, naked in the sun
that finds him rocking the gold statuette
of Victory, placed by the horn of Ammon;
the Red Sea's dredged for pearls to spot his room.
Whoever marries him must thread the net
of red and purple he throws at the moon –
Octavia died, a blade in her gullet.

The fire that gutted Rome, fanned by a wind
that stoked the blaze to a red tidal wave,
was at his instigation. In their minds
men have already placed him in a grave
the crow struts over. Things are upside down,
gold sand for wrestlers comes in place of wheat,
naumachias demand monsters from the deep
to be salvaged by a carnival fleet,
Africa and India scoured for beasts
smashed up like firewood – the Emperor can't sleep,
so must be entertained until the sand
in the arena's troughed with blood. He feasts
on peacocks encased in goldleaf, and stands,
divine exemplar of the human beast.

Profanation of every rite decrees
an inauspicious death. Men drown their words
like stones; each week a new conspiracy's
unearthed, the plotters killed before they're heard,
their heads are packed into an apple-bin –
even Seneca's had to renounce life,
his riches the Emperor's gratuity.
In Rome it doesn't pay to be a wife
who mourns a husband for she joins his pyre:

our only common law is treachery.
Paranoid, flanked by Mazacian horsemen,
nibbling aphrodisiacs to refire
his spent member, the song-bird in his den
thinks only of night. Lust heats like a wire.

Tyrant follows tyrant on thinning ice,
and each at last plunges to the black pool
to solidify. New taxes, new vice,
supersede before the old corpse can cool.
Nero, deserted by the army, ran
to some outlying villa, unprepared
for death, dusty, his silk clothes burred with thorns,
his unskilled sword-hand trembling and his scared
eyes appealing for respite. It took two
hands to assist him with the knife, his torn
windpipe gouting blood. The mob would have flayed
him alive, trussed and pitched him in a sack
into the Tiber. Now Galba's arrayed
in purple, men wish the old tyrant back.

Height: average, rarely used to good effect,
the body pustular, pitted with sores,
the features without singular defect,
but epicene, profuse sweat in the pores.
Eyes sea-blue, dwarfed by pupils, myopic,
neck squat on a pepperpot torso,
belly already slackly protuberant,
legs spindly, hair dyed gold, the voice a slow
drawl quickly mounting to hysterical
passion, eyelids pasted with indigo.
Histrionic, his one pursuit pleasure,
facetious, inordinately jealous,
hell-bent, I itemise his faults to cure
the harsh exile of one Sosianus.

LATE YEAR FOG

They're stacked above the tideline, lobster pots
wintering in the cove. The fishermen
have beached their dinghies, flipped them upside down
for rain to pummel. Now mist drops again,

obscuring the backdrop to a dead year,
its dissolute links eroded, its spark
a coal patinated in grainy ash.
The wires are down, a taxi hunts the dark,

laying out traces for a small hotel
couched in its cat's-cradle of country lanes –
the white hart on its sign jumps with the wind,
and with a clatter rights itself again.

Turned soil, high hedges, and diffused droplets
of mist silvering, now a tractor's sway
weaves lurchingly out to menace traffic,
its tailboard unlit, it at last gives way

caterpillaring down a hairfine track
to a loaf-shaped farm and its fuzz of thatch.
The dark's a thistlehead, in a call-box
cold hands flick for a number with a match,

but can't get through. The year's dying in thin
voices cabled beneath the sea, a man
coddled by bourbon speaks to someone here
from a snowed-in loft high in Manhattan,

snow-ploughs shunting the drifts to yellow waste.
The taxi's found its scent, its red brake-lights
work hard on the spiral descent to where
a country inn is half absorbed by night

and half lit up, it bears a holly wreath
interleaved with ivy and mistletoe.
Someone slams a log and its embers flush
from a blue wood-ash to an orange glow.

HOUSES WE NEVER LIVE IN

We've learnt to mark them on a mental chart
with the detail of a map-maker's art,
the ones we would have lived in, a thatched barn
awaiting conversion, screened by a wood,
its hay-loft a natural poet's eyrie,
or that time near Shelley, a fishing lodge
on a bottle-glass green reach of the Stour,
and somewhere, a deserted rectory,
rook garrulous, crow querulous, the mood
conditioned by a squat yew fed on blood
at Nayesbury, iconoclastic roundheads
looting the chapel, poling the stained glass
to violet ice of a fragmented lake.
And always houses screened off by a drive
of cerise rhododendrons, an outline
of white or red stone with gabled turrets
glimpsed in passing, the late afternoon shine
burning gold in a high window. Always,
the many lost, a windmill on a plain,
seen from the car that day of sparkling rain,
a Tudor farmhouse with uneven floors,
a corn-mill, places taken in en-route
as imaginary refuges, while we
hold to the leaf-crowned road, stare at closed doors,
choose a house a village – a private game,
refurbish rooms, light lamps, and change the name.

MARBLES

Cool to the hand, an early memory:
our parquet floor made for fluidity –

a polished surface on which we'd compete
for coloured marbles in our stockinged feet,

the chalky, opalescent whites, a twist
of scarlet in crystal an adept wrist

would release for the strike, a navy blue
chipped from long service, its unusual hue

lent to it a prestige, an old warhorse,
stabled, unleashed only on the right course,

pocketed, coveted, and lodged inside
a velvet bag; we played against a tide

of domestic complaint, our galaxy
of coloured suns held its ascendancy

over the court of adults, meteorites,
explosive supernovas, stars in flight,

prismatic twinklings, the imagined spark
as a tiger's eye hummed to find its mark

in a green whorl intersected by pink,
the impact had it teeter on the brink

of the skyline, ricochet from the flash
before disorbiting in a weird dash…

Our games created war amongst the stars,
the cratered minerals, diamond-rayed pulsars,

little moon maps, or multicoloured eyes,
shifting their place in the unstable skies.

MY FATHER'S MODELS

Glue from the wing-struts of a Tiger Moth;
you worked with a watchmaker's precision
at assembling models ostensibly
for my edification – it was yours,

the pleasure in the delayed completion,
the last coat of paint – I still remember
how you contrived to fashion a Junker
from metal splinters of a crashed aircraft

that shriekingly nosedived into the dunes.
These models were realities for you,
impractical exhibits I could touch,
but never use. They had become a craft

you practised in unsociably late hours,
leaving the varnished exhibit for me
to discover assembled on its mount,
the whisky vaporised in the decanter…

Mostly estrangement, our divergent lives
went wide of a pretended harmony,
and once seeing my father in the street,
and out of context, I could only run

for fear it wasn't him nose up against
a shop window. It's his face I recall
superimposed on mine in the mirror,
directing my shaving hand, a blood fleck

like a red eye in a white carnation.
Dark moods, I'd stay down in a sea-hollow,
only to be found out. Who was that man
made me return, instinctively follow?

Today at an airport, I find myself
recollecting planes to the last detail;
the one I broke, tried to conceal, and found
to my relief, restored, with a new tail.

BUGGING

Flotillas of mobile algae
        jerkily rotate in this pond,
cellular units too small for the eye,
        spherical, globular, concealed by frond –
whip-like flagellums, swimming hairs, they cross
        an oval pool the green of moss.

Survivors named from Greek legend,
        one-eyed, multi-armed, they compose
a tableau of monsters, features that lend
        a meaning to anatomies that rose
out of a fabled cave or marsh, tiny
        organisms, the water flea's

cyclopean eye, feelered head,
        the somersaulting hydra's tree
of tentacles, the water-bear, the red
        projectile of the stick-insect's body,
these are the erinyes that police the maze
        of a weed forest's sluggish haze.

The pond-skater on the surface
        rows leisurely, while on its back
the water boatman's listening to trace
        the vibrational pitch of fry and track
the source to an extinction – a black-out
        eclipses the newly hatched trout.

Nothing's safe in this bug empire,
        the diving beetle's torpedo
is no match for the tadpole; the red fire
        of a newt blazes from blue-indigo.
Then quiet, shadows like a panther's skin,
            deepen, as the thunder slams in.

POND SKATERS

Tension transmits a buzz to the surface,
duckweed flotillas buoy where a fine lace

of insects microdot the clear shallows.
A reed casts the imprint of a gallows

over a water-measurer's galley,
bridge-struts paralleling its nibbed body;

the whirligig beetle's circular spin
describes the dance of filings to a pin,

but it's the pond skaters' inverse shadows
filmed on the still skeins of the undertow,

in black clusters of spots, engage the eye,
before one sees them resting on the sky

reflected in the water's lens. They wait
for flies to tumble into the surfeit

of surface-drift – look: this one's light body
is upheld by the water's buoyancy,

the bristle-pads on its legs move so quick
across a plane of glass, each dimpled flick

is cushioned like a hoof on springy soil.
It retrieves a fly out of the blue oil,

its lifeguard's grip creates a stranglehold
on a victim that crackles, green and gold,

a pyre of shimmer – and is rowed behind
an island of frond, a green slatted blind

runs with a wind-glance, and a midge shower
dance as the light rays form a sunflower.

FERMENTATION

The pond's the colour of an old carp's skin,
a blue-green filamental algae spawns
so quickly that the dragonfly's hairpin –

a bronze totem-pole with an Inca mask
of ocelli looks like a hovercraft
above a slick of weed. A water cask

scummed over, it's the green of apple moss
on rush leaves, the brown rat's bony midden
is particled into a scaly dross

of fish-bones, feathers, fur, a sparrow's head.
Their highroads lead from the pond to a barn,
a scored run. Sunlight picks out every thread

in the silver-horned caddis fly, its black
and white curling antennae are a stag's –
antlers, head lowered, sweeping to attack,

its steel-blue wings scintillate in the light.
A day in late summer, each brilliant
that travels through the water is in flight,

the wood-mouse scavenges hazels, rose-hips,
and chisels an oval hole through each nut.
A sudden splash and it's a moorhen flips

wide of the shadow of a hawk. It dives.
We take the gold-down from the mellow light,
we'll need it when the first redwing arrives.

AN OLD SCORE

An ox-eyed twist in each nubby conker –
veteran antagonists, one partially
withstanding a hairline segmentary flaw,
I still remember the finality

with which mine cracked, after its gnarled black shell
had been championed through three winters, the split
was like a glass exploding under heat,
a detonation that your perfect hit

followed through, the backlash grazing your thumb…
The prickly pods are down again, I pass
the stone farmhouse that you inherited
from generations on the land, the grass

is burnished with a fall of chestnut leaves.
You're working somewhere on a drainage ditch
through a beech copse, clearing out wedged black leaves
that block the flow, boarding out where a hitch

could have a rain-flooded steam overflow.
Ten years? I cuff a chestnut to a shine,
highlighting silver in that squirrel-red,
and darker hues of mahogany, wine,

the raindrop berried in a thrush's eye,
and feel again the urge to make things crack,
to level with you, sharpening my aim,
feet squarely spaced, wrist flexing to attack.

SPACE FACILITATOR

He paints: a brush-tip not an aerosol
        adding depth to blue heptagons,
the cobalt deserts of deep space.
Since he came back to earth from a black hole,
        the time-warp's blocked his memory,
and when the flashes come he's still up there
in the orbital band for geostationary
        satellites, holding a fixed place
by swinging round the world's revolutions,
before the fissure opened, and his mind
        closed down at the enormity.
He monitors space debris, satellites
gone defunctive, bodies, equipment lost
        that no reclamation patrol
can locate – fuel-tanks, missile-casings, tools,
the metal wheel of potential fall-out
        conflagrating before it cools
on impact with the earth, the sea. He writes
reports rejected for their literary
        content, evidence of a century
consigned to archives. He is lonelier
than the first man, and awaits the return
        of someone liberated from a past
accessible to both. Time moves too fast,
and the last one to come back was charred to ash
        by some detonative fuel flash.
He dreams of those above who didn't burn,
        lost in indefinite orbit,
and how his contemporaries might get free
of the great rift, the cosmic trap and find
        re-entry to the stratosphere,
occur as a collective flock one night,
preserved, helmeted, touching down
        like migrant birds attracted to a light.

TERRORISTS

They dyed their hair platinum and drove red
sports models across Flatland, a new state
created for a species invented
by holographic insemination –
light-people whose infiltration
threatened film-archives, they were illusions
in 3D who'd acquired a permanence,
and coloured like exotic butterflies
in red and blue and violet
undermined governments. They were the spies
of photographic records, and pursued,
adopted additional dimensions
and grew invisible to the fixed eye.
Projected on to children born in space,
they became a universal menace –
an elusive race spreading to Washington,
and by degrees identified, a face,
the blue pulsation of a light pattern.

The terrorists were Warhol creations,
monosyllabic, casual to the point
of mindless dissociation.
They concealed guns inside tape-recorders,
and treated language as demonstrative
of a retarded species. Their orders
were radio-transmitted in a code
they deciphered with silicone. They drove
all night across Flatland startling a herd
of square-bodied cattle from square meadows,
their radar-scans picking up on a bird
kiting the night skies, but the hologram
people had turned invisible, a blue,
a violet flicker shifting out of view
were hints of their dispersal. They turned round
and faced a flat horizon, a flat road,
abandoned their cars, set up a flat stone
to a flat god and prayed without a sound.

BLUE LAGOON

Your dresses spilled across a hotel bed
were like the hectic dispersal of flame
wind-smashed tulips leave – overblown goblets
cracked into volutes – yellow, violet, red,

rouge brushed on orange, a translucent pink…
Your monogrammed silver combs and hairbrush
were childhood things breath-printed by the maid
who shadow-waltzed with your clothes after drink

had fired her to filch perfume, blunt the nib
of a shaped lipstick, while you sunned below,
prostrate in the pressurised wall of heat,
blue love-bites lozenging a hip, a rib,

your halved bikini emphasising how
the briefest triangle of white remains
an isthmus between two reaches of tan.
90 in the shade. A dead tidal flow…

Your Japanese lover's black kimono
was old-world silk; withdrawn, unwesternised,
he wore white make-up and restrained your flight
into the wheel-spin of a casino.

Storminess broke you. He was gone before
the late summer calm hatched a dragon's egg,
and equinoctial winds folded surf
in white thunder sheets across the foreshore.

Wild-eyed from too many mid-afternoon
aperitifs, you stayed on, a last guest –
hair a blond ruckus, facing out to sea,
drinking your favourite cocktail, Blue Lagoon.

FARMDOG

Hot nares to its greying snout,
was a snuffling shambles of awkward joints
in the sun, the belly gone bald
as a pig's, the fleas crackling in its coat,
splayed in the farmyard, shadow floating out
like wrack in slow eddies, but alert
to each footstep, ears pricked, territorial
aggression asserted at a bound,
the bark vociferating menace, and up
would trail one the length of the lane,
bring a cyclist down and agitate, teeth
bared, the snarl of it twisted
from the larynx with the congested shriek
of an engine coming to life after
the zero-freeze of inaction. Old scars,
cat-bites, nose-knouts, did nothing to deter
its officious policing of strangers,
a black moors-dog, bred with a Doberman,
blooded this bull-necked mongrel's
baying truculence. Branch-clouts, a gun-shot,
its temerity survived the lot,
and was nursed back to a new ferocity,
its jaws set at one's ankles like a trap.
Muzzled for the postman, the tradesman,
survived without being put down, tenure
it got as right of the survivor,
to outlive its owner, see a third son dead,
and intrepidly claim new privileges,
a yellow-toothed assertion of its future.

A VISIT

The country bus idled at every stop,
incestuous gossip, news of a crop
curtailed by the indifferent summer heat.
We flagged on, branches flailing at the roof

and windows, logged to a slow motion crawl
by a tractor and its jolting trailer
indomitably holding to the crown.
It lurched off without signals, bull-snorting,

rattling its gruff claptrap into a lane.
At the penultimate stop, jostling cows
were filing out of a field to their sheds.
Engine off, arms folded, we watched them led

across the road, and frisked into a yard.
A manor house with its cascading red
swirl of overblown roses, a farmstead,
then cherry trees screening yours from the road,

an early 19th, pinkish-grey granite
farmhouse, its agapanthus and sun-dial,
its converted library a square barn,
rooms filled with the incomplete inventory

of your books, Persian carpets, rarities
of an orientalist, your thin beard
straggled into an ash-grey waterfall,
a line of curling smoke. A tortoise snaps

the black heart from a pansy while we sit
and feel the warm air colour on our skin.
Your land stretches on every side, courgettes
have ripened, lettuce, orange marrow flowers,

the scarlet bean-flowers spiral like sweetpeas.
Everything's here; I stay on until dark.
A squibbing mosquito whines round the room,
blood-hungry to inflict its red scorch-mark.

CHANGES

You're under glass. Inconsistent seasons
have made this an expediency, the farm's
a hothouse aquarium of tomatoes,
sweetpeas, carnations, crops that caused alarm

exposed to the chameleonic skies
of an island climate. Broad of beam now,
the years have weathered your youthful figure;
you're patient in the yard with a lame cow,

your big hands bony, knobbled like a branch.
We've lost our thread now that I'm much away,
what can a poet do in the stack-yard,
boxing seed-potatoes or baling hay

our youth survives, the present is a gap?
Returning imposes a new exile,
rootless feet drifting through the countryside,
electric fencing has replaced your stile . . .

Homecoming means an appraisal of years,
most marry in a small community,
and if they questioned what a line can do,
the only answer is it sets one free . . .

The faces swim, they nose past me like fish
browsing the glass, tentative, uncertain,
in this game of who identifies who.
I'm thankful for the dicing autumn rain,

abrupt showers that leave the lanes open,
three hours' hard walking with no one around,
the sky silvering from a bean-grey sea,
my mind hunting a thread I haven't found

by the time I take the herring-skin sheened
hill-slope to your farm. You're loading a truck,
and make a valedictory gesture,
part dismissal and part waving good luck.

CROWS IN A MISTY FIELD

Vociferous, came down barking outrage,
a querulous fidgety assertion
of field rights – a heckled raucous mewling
that had drifts flap up in staggered wingbeats,
a ragged shuttlecock-feathered heavy
lift in their sooty numbers to an oak.
Others stayed down in the blown pink chiffon,
skeins of autumnal mist unstrung by wind,
then reunited, bushes of blue smoke.
I stood still waiting for them to regroup,
a coven's exchange of imprecations,
a tetchy silence, contested side-shifts,
before their pot-bellied resolution
had them stake out a territorial claim,
reminding of their primeval tenure,
their mortmain of carrion since the beginning –
a crow facing the first planetary light,
a black silhouette against the orange.
One wheeled up in an arc and was pursued,
undercut by another in the timed
contiguous chase of two butterflies,
and planed down, marking out the dribble-eyed,
nose-reddened hare dead on that scuffed fallow,
stiff with it, toxic chemicals, and stood
in a near circle, a burial party
in black mourning, cautious inquisitors,
waiting to tear out eyeball and sinew,
spade in like trenchermen. I left them there,
vigilant surgeons on a deserted field,
a blood-orange sun sitting in blue mist,
ebullient, irreproveable shapes,
sure of their find and unwilling to scare.

ELM LOAD

Puddling its reflection a chimney pot
has formed a watercolour on the road,
shadows are miniaturists tinting there.
A lorry crane keeps dipping for its load

of sawn-up elm trunks, a petrol chain-saw
has sharked through the hedgerow, its high-pitched whine
an outboard motor worked at full throttle.
The bark's rimed seaweed-green, the end discs shine –

circles of white in which the grain's rough-edged.
They've felled with few omissions in a lane
whose gradient winds leisurely to crossroads.
The sawdust's sherbet-yellow in the rain,

big flakes that dust the earth packed around roots,
gone dead on the quickening blast of sap
that shaped the warped branch-twistings into light.
Trees in their upward drive form a veined map,

each arterial highway leading to space,
a windy crown. At each field entrance wood
is stacked for loading. A dead rabbit lies
stiff in the act of running, a dark blood

has haemorrhaged in one eye and bibbed the fur.
A dog will drag it by the nape and lay
it out – a sodden mat upon the lawn.
Elms in their roped up stash are greenish-grey,

split down they'll feed the fires of a county,
the sap still sizzle. Here they are on view,
pig-heavy segments cracked like worn leather.
Laid out horizontally they're untrue

to their vertical stance. It is an end.
One must grow accustomed to how the light
falls without interruption, the sunset
a clearer scarlet prelude to the night.

MOTH-TRAPPER

A moth-trapper's vapour-bulb shows tonight,
a blue illumination in the wood,
gaudy wings hit the baffles and subside
as a floral paisley in egg-cartons,
a fauna of tiger, red-underwing,
a cream-bordered green-pea, the dazzle-flight
of hawk-moths; brittle silks come from the hood
of leaf canopy to enquire how light
has formed a global planet in the dark,
a fixed hypnotic point for wings to tap,
dusting the cone with filigree; the man
observes them spot, concealed behind rough bark.

We watch him from our own side of the glass,
looking out on a night interpreted
through long familiarity with things.
A breeze picks out a slack chord in the grass,
and in imagining moth-flakes we find
their impulse has equivalents in the mind,
a lost centre we gravitate towards
but never reach. It's curiosity
holds us to life and feeds us to the flame.
We draw back from a smokiness of breath.
At dawn the man's hands will be powdered gold,
his eye selective in its scrutiny,
freeing the known, finding for one a name.

THE GRAND TOUR

A field of bluebells shot through with stitchwort,
and now the chestnut candles pink and white,
birches are fragrant with rose, and a trap
loops up an avenue, its steaming flight

brought to a canter as the lanterns pool.
The stable boys don't recognise Pushkin,
his negroid lips, olive face, staggered hair,
his finger browsing on the diamond pin

that checks his silk cravat. Tonight he'll read
in the crystal library; deliver lines
censored by Benckendorff's spies, pick a rose,
and hold it out to a girl whose eyes shine

with mauve-shot sapphire, close his book and leave,
his coat-tails flying. Dead under the Tsars,
their faces stare out of beige photographs –
their eyes are fixed like the permanent stars,

Baratynsky, Lermontov, Polonsky…
names travelling like birch leaves across a plain,
poets on tour from house to house, white-faced,
monocle, arriving out of the rain.

Rilke in a Prague bookshop, Baudelaire
fogged out in Brussels, Lorca evoking
Andalusia to a student-group,
their delivery lost outside the ring

of those who gathered, intent on the word.
A pre-recording age, we give their voice
the modulated speech-rhythms that fit
our way of reading, or concede the choice

to a contemporary at a microphone,
the trans-Atlantic poet, jet-lagged, tired,
baring his isolation to the crowd,
his voice off-key, metallic, underwired.

PACTS

With most, the secrecy's a double life,
a wolf-shadow, the invisible vein
lost in the choking multiplicity
of ivy, and renewed over again
by black water of its underground source,
an ice-chilled runnel untouched by the sun,
the bottomless unmirrored reservoir.

Singular or obsessive, what is done
won't disappear, and so is returned to,
the assignation that leads to blackmail,
the degradation of a man broken
by something stronger than himself, turned out
to founder on the surface of his skin.
Men try to take their secrets into death,
a black butterfly mounted on a pin.

With some the pact's between glass and bottle,
whisky measures with no constraining count,
the impulse terrible at night, alone.
Duplicities, the need to keep concealed
the unshareable, weighted with a stone.
Love, fraud, the signature upon a line,
irrevocable in its consequence,
the daily battle with the blind cave-fish,
consigning it to a dark location.

Those who get through must follow to the end,
breast the cold stream, or face up to a wall,
become themselves or it in the exchange
at death; the captive out is it despatched
or judged, animal running through the hall,
dislaired, identified, the knowledge clear
both of its resilience and its fall.

ELDER WINE

Timothy grass and cow parsley
silked by the wind; head cradled back
in verticals of green, I lay,
an insect supine on the track,

unable to regain balance,
carapace grained by jags of straw,
while over me a thistle flower
was kneaded by a kitten's paw –

a bluetit crammed its craw with seeds.
Lethargy of the white June day
saturated with elder flowers
mustily scented as red may,

its surf of colour faded to
bitty pinks of sweet william.
Coolness was the flagged wine-cellar,
wine fermentation, damson jam…

We picked white flowers for unguents,
creamy umbels with bitter leaves,
a recipe for complexion,
grass burs hung seed-spores on our sleeves,

and by midday, standing stirrup
on the farm hill we'd hear the tick
of the postman's unserviced bike,
no brakes, to hedge-crash was the trick…

Late summer saw our fingers mauve
from berrying, the violet pitch
of ripenesss weighed the elders down,
rose-hips ripened by the ditch.

Commemorative with new bottles,
we drank last season's cool black wine,
watching how light restored to it,
returned the berry's purple shine.

BABEL

Stone flighted conically towards the sky –
a word-tower extending from a poet's mouth
to the sun; vision the dream of language

and its dispersal.
And always the vibration: the seamless word
alive to the animals under trees,
the river directed by the salmon's dictates,
flowers instructed as lovers by bees.

And whether of stone or light it stood, and
they came across deserts to hear
the universal resonance.

When the poet couldn't sustain the dream
it crashed. Light was translated back to stone
and the fall smashed a hollow
in the earth; thunder reverberated.
The animals fled and were individualised –

and those tribes who survived the shock
ran and articulated screams
and each recognised their disunity –
brother and sister and lover

and were never again one when they spoke to each other.

ALL THE PRESIDENT'S MEN

Back from the dogdays – leafy interludes
in green oases – Maine, Connecticut,
jacuzzis thinning tension, bright oil spots
worked by the masseur's fingers to a glow,

whisky igniting duodenal pain,
the fagged, dehydrated pores thirst for rain,
the cleansing shower; the fall's vermilion flame.
'Benny, they say half Asia's disappeared',

'Well, that's sure news' and then the bugged lift halts
and someone walks their creases down the floor.
'If Franny knew about that backroom-bar,
that negro kid just dancing in a star,

his phallus first a python, then a trunk,
and free for all ... Fran's dieticians think
her figure will cut free from gelatine.
Half Asia missing, and you need a drink...'

He lifts his General Custer paperweight
into his hand; the model astronaut
stares from a KGB's *Who's Who*.
Two months ago, there was news of a fault,

a leak involving a call-girl, and now
the topfloor suite is under surveillance,
the last two Presidents are blocked in ice,
stored there as aquarium exhibits...

Today the students demonstrate with guns;
someone is describing Natasha's tits,
and how three men chicken-pecked caviar
from her silicone convexities.

When Benny calls, it's to say reprisals
are under way: 'Florida's in the sea.
The President can't be reached.' 'What you say?'
'Champagne not bourbon. This is history.'

AIDS

Each of us has contrived a secret place
to bury that word, dispense with the fear
by meeting it in individual ways
below the surface.
                       We're not right at all
in youth or age, the uncut flower, the full
which lives in its perfection like a rose.
We're under threat. The faces that I know
are cautious, not diminished, but conscious
of being vulnerable; the universal shadow
tilts on each city. It could be me –
no matter that I've kept the word hidden,
pretending always that it's someone else
a stranger must address –
diagnosing a state, an abstract death,
malignant, irreversible. Who's free?

I see you fish-ghosting a shop window,
friend of my youth, iller, older,
still the same frightened child beneath.
I won't enquire, rather go out and celebrate
how first mauve crocuses command the light;
and how the coast we knew and know is there,
lavender as the shower moves in – Good Luck –

all of us need it everywhere.

LOVE AND DEATH

They're much the same; the fear of one
involves the other – locket on a chain
cushioned in white satin,
is worn to match the ivy leaf at last
in a French cemetery under rain,
fragrant with lilacs, allysum, tenebrous yews,
and if the link is inextricable,
so the intensity's doubled, passion
flaming like a ship lividly ablaze
on black night waters, while the punctual ray
of a lighthouse searches like a white stick
for a connection. Not elegiac,
but trying for a dimension
reached through the ballistics of orgasm,
and transported beyond the physical,
is how we come to reconcile our lives
with touch and leave, awareness of a fragility
that has us lift a torch out of the fire,
shock-headed, roaring red faggot,
and carry it across the beach
at twilight under violet and green skies,
straining again towards the high point of desire.

INVISIBLE CITIES

The landmarks grow less permanent, a place
becomes the evocation of its recent past
to each new generation, a city
built over by a city, palimpsest,
penumbra of the sunflower's rag-doll face
that brightened childhood, pin-cushion for bees.
It's all deception, an illusory
retrieval of what's lost that makes a street
significant, peculiarly our own,
after the highrise increments, the loss
of a wild rose garden, the cobbled maze
that was a labyrinthine way to school,
we stare at what has vanished, and it's there
again, blindingly real, the house we knew,
white walls and shutters, its doors painted blue,

a home compact in the imaginary
province from which we're inevictable,
our one fortified irreducible country.
The world's unshareable, we see by age
with no common convergence, see the dross
or innovations, and both are the same
in not belonging to the singular
moment in which we saw for the first time
and came to know a white cat, seek a lime
for its garden shade, find a friend's house by
a green paint splinter in the door, explore
a precinct that seemed like a continent,
now disappeared for thru-roads, an architecture

translated by how we meet the future?

FLAUBERT

An ursine gait. At thirty he's fifty;
the protuberant eyes are like a squid's
mounted above a bulldog's jowl;
his blond walrus-moustache contains more hair

than the ermine dress-collar on a coat.
He is stoutly provincial, boorishly
unflattering in company;
he places Rouen round him like a moat,

and reads de Sade because the book lacks trees.
His craft demands a watchmaker's
diamond precision; killing assonance,
he regroups words; volume, colour and sound

are reappraised until *le mot juste* shines.
It is a pyramid he builds with lines,
searching more for a colour than a plot,
the purple of Salammbô, wood-louse grey

of Madame Bovary. He writes til dawn,
the endless work-notes, and his shaded lamp
is a navigating light to bargemen
pushing a course towards the orange East

detonating above the star-shot Seine.
Work is his antidote against slow-rot,
the syphilitic strain he treats with lead.
At forty his leonine voice still roars

for his mother to bring him milk in bed.
The disappointed satyr in him rears
its phallic horns; his desk is the dust-bowl
of an arena without spectators.

Head-down, untiring still, at 3 a.m.
he tries unsparingly for perfection.
Ambition's a rusty anchor; his art's
controlled by the incisive selection

of a Byzantine jeweller's eye.
The days are routinal, he's in a zoo-
compound, a Carthaginian elephant
deciding on a mauve, a gold, a blue.

SNAKE FIGHT

The stone's incandescent. By noon it burns
to the intensity of rock cooling
from a meteoric split-off. Heat turns

the gritty sand to a firewalker's coals.
Something's racing round the hub of a wheel,
an indigo snake jockeys, veers in, rolls,

then rapidly describes a circle round
a vigilant diamondback rattlesnake,
its blunt head periscoping from the ground

in a tensely vibrating S; its force
contained in the triggered head's bullet-strike
of needling fangs. The other holds its course,

widening then contracting that beat, it's like
a big cat closing on petrified prey,
while vultures stand off and a red-backed shrike

loads its beak with sinew. Now nose to nose,
the two confront; the indigo's too quick,
and sidesteps the aimed head, it will not close

until its opponent's too tired to track
its blinding, unpredictable rhythm;
the lozenges catch fire along its back.

The tail-tip rattles thrash a crescendo,
the straightened body aims wide of its mark,
the forked tongue flickering; the indigo's

the inert one now, instinct slows its run.
Beady eyes, open mouthed, its energy
a withheld bolt, it shoots in with the sun

behind it, mouth clamped to its victim's head,
teeth working through the brain, it won't let go
until the diamondback is laid out dead;

the last tremor expired. Then it will eat,
ingorge the slack body's iridescence,
unhurried, growing bloated in the heat.

BATHROOM SCENE

Wristwatch off, silk shirts, your head slanting back
beneath a regulated eye-dropper –
your bathroom scene, mirrors frosted with steam,
a cologne bottle minus its stopper;

the tumbler of Jack Daniels packed with ice,
two open novels face down on the floor,
your mind lit up by days of travelling,
your clothes already trailing in a spoor

from room to room – garments acid with sweat,
your booty locked in the Moroccan case –
an heirloom with a faded monogram.
I'd speak to you through the slant door, a vase

of scented blue irises in one hand,
a green towel in the other, cigarettes
for the traveller's mosquito-riddled nerves;
your grizzled stubble gone, features reset

to meet the enquiring aesthetic eye…
Your stories laid a zigzag powder trail,
the fulminations too many; you seemed
like someone holding on to a ship's rail

to steady the storm inside; it would take
weeks before you synthesised what you'd found,
your voice still rattled by the whirring blades
of a helicopter low to the ground,

climbing to clear a belt of rainforest.
Knowledge of the interior? … You stand
and face the mirror; what's inside comes back,
the whisky tumbler clatters from your hand…

BLUEPRINT

Five flights up, white-suited, he scans the town,
his tie bridges his shoulder, a rainbow
the wind has blown back in a violet arc.
The highrise landscape glitters – pane by pane
transmitting a wheat-ear blond glow.
His eye takes in the fish-tanks then looks down
at what we've lost, the earth that's capped
by a metallic concrete shell,
the worn out drum-skin of a century
written in tyre-treads, oil stains, and now mapped
out in the reaches of deep space.
Nettles have broken through a dead surface,
a shock of green asserting somewhere growth
goes on independent of man.
He's here to envisage a future plan
to accommodate the denaturalised –
man's uninstinctive colonies
waiting to leave the planet, facing blanks
beyond the Planck wall – stellar vibrancy?
Everywhere ash-stains mark the old forests,
a universe without a tree.

His eyes drop to a turquoise swimming-pool.
A speaker transmits a tracked quasar beat.
Two leather figures dance there to the stars,
and have raided the ice-burials to eat
a species they don't recognise.
He goes back in; the torrid heat
has burnt his skin, expended cars
rust to their hulks; the earth's a skeleton
lost to memory like the mastodon,
buried, with its survivors in retreat.

SAMARITANS

The cupped receiver's a confessional,
the subject is myself, yet when I speak
it's with a detached commentary – the leak
concerns a stranger I objectify
to someone that I never really knew,
and have a thinning link with. Survival
would seem to be the question, for I've lost
the current which electrifies, the wire
that sparks inside the head.

                        I try
to imagine features to suit the voice
that persuades me towards the practical,
the rational alternatives
to being caught inside a trap,
a sort of wicker-shuttered lobster-pot
that's closed over me – it is dark in there,
the groundswell is too turbulent
to allow for stability, a claw
rattles the one light-chinking flaw,
a life-wish, death-trap, possibilities?...

My head is lighter but the dark won't clear,
and all over the city those whose fear
is uncontainable show up as lights
pulsing on a switchboard, urgent flashes.
Two strangers, our transient connection
brought a still eye to the black storm,
a suspension of dilemma: the night
is full of voices, someone else somewhere
will follow on from me, we are night moths
singed by the flame and still facing that flare.

TRANSSEXUAL

A rickety table
in a dilapidated studio,
the poster of Garbo's
a reinvocation of *l'âge d'or*
Hollywood Highs, a lipstick bow's
delineated indigo –

impossible to imitate
in poverty, the gelid room
with its opulent gilt mirror
from which a disapproving face
stares back in terror
where the stubble shows blue-lavender

through matt foundation.
Lipstick tubes, plastic razor,
a gold Bardot wig on its stand,
brushed and lacquered, it's the day
brings interminable ennui.
Night is a source of money –

selling out on a body,
arranging deals in alleyways,
always the fear, always the fear –
a miscalculated assignation,
informer or psychopath,
pusher burning for a stashed cache,

there's no retribution…
She reads a magazine at dusk
on fashion-tips. The blue turns black.
She checks her make-up, locks the door,
learns to balance on her heels.
There might be no coming back.

BROTHELS

They too are a house of call. No longer
sumptuously baroque, with scarlet sofas
and flowered wall-panels imitating
        coromandel lacquer,
that spurious intimacy gone,
of disarray, waspies, liquor,
the unlacing to copiousness of flesh,
Renoir's pink-gold, voluminous axes,
        a kitten with a twist of string,
occupied in a corner; a basket
of fruit left untouched on the mantelpiece;
        pineapple, peaches, a still-life,
green-polished apples, black grapes like lockets,
the girl called Sabine.
        A post-Goncourt age
has eliminated the stage –
beauty; the wolf pursues the lioness
with more discretion and no less
        fear of disease,
always the lonely stair, the uncertain
fear of a trap, the face in the mirror,
part agonised, but overruled
by anticipation, expectancy
of the small room, stiletto-heeled stranger,
        the prelude to the encounter,
more than the act, and the recognition
in the dazed, lonely return to the street,
not of remorse, but division,
        the time held secret, put aside
to an unshareable memory,
something separate and kept alive like that
through decades of change, remembered at death,
        the three dead roses in a tiny flat.

REVOCATION

With starker issue, days come to a halt,
the bad end of the year when a red sun
declines by four, its afterglow,
a volcano's molten fire-core,
a planetary upheaval that stays
to warm our universal fault,
but for these dark months has withdrawn its light.

Last leaves on the willow blacken,
its fronds are a porcupine's quills
backcombed into a thinning straw;
the things we say and do lessen
in their intensity, a hibernative
impulse reduces everything
to slow down, hang on, and survive
these worst days in a primal trance.

It is a time when the mind registers
its losses, records faces gone
about the world, and never to return,
a time when the hands invite flame
to read in their reflection the story
of the masked dance, the hunted animal,
and if crossing a bridge at dusk you find
a greatcoated man shredding a letter
into an undulant river,
his act of revocation times with how
we leave the year behind, and fortified
by whisky shots walk out into the snow.

THE VARIOUS WAYS

A Lamborghini flies through a dust storm,
the driver's blue shades offset the harsh light
radiated from burnt lavender fields.
His momentum will take him through the night,

silent towns aquatinted by rivers,
pastel houses floating water colours
into patchy mill-pond stills in current;
a girl waves from a window at his car.

His fingers thrum with anticipation
at each delay, cattle blocking a road.
It's news of his divorce has him tighten,
the pulse in his head threatens to explode.

It is her face he drives toward, black trees
contort, someone flags him down to a halt.
A goat's given birth on the road, a youth
defends that raw flesh from a swarm of bees.

CÉZANNE

A native recklessness; the eye controls
      the inner equilibrium
of colour, imparts with simplicity,
the dynamics of hidden energy
in objects quiet by their grouping, here
      the burning lacquer red
of an apple's asymmetrical sphere,
flushes from a yellow twist, and is thrown
into highlight by a black wine bottle;
      a green pot arrests cadmium,
its terracotta speaking of the earth.
La nature morte, arranged on a white cloth;
the endless permutations make it clear
      how each time we see, we give birth
to an object that's still familiar,
but redimensionalised by the light
of an interior plane, so it is sight
      that's variable and nature shaped
by its mobility. Obsessively,
those mental satellites recur; violent
green apples, pears, a lemon, banded cup,
      and stare at us with the silent
captivation of things that realise
the rightness of their placing. A black clock
stands without hands, provoking the carmine
      of a triton shell's sensuous
orifice, red on the outside, a mouth
that calls attention by its shock
to the subdued components of the room.
      Each new summary sweep of tones,
impresses by its finding in napkins,
pitchers, silver, glass, tints the Venetians
used to illuminate the allegory
      of myth, the Ovidian
transference of identity. Cézanne's
rugged determination got it right,

finding in the ordinary, the light
      that centres as a silver ring
on a wine-glass, and creates a wheat-field
in a baguette supporting a bread-knife.
Right to the end, insulted, it was life
      he celebrated, while children
threw stones at his shabby clothes in the street,
and he, walking out to his studio,
pockets bulging, knew how the beautiful
      is inherent in all that lives,
and once externalised in its true form,
remains as that, the green cooking apple
transmuted to the spatial, mirrors back
the light, by which altering it survives.

DISCOVERIES

We climbed by nightfall to the island's peak.
The plateau beneath us showed one
tree twisted into agonised antlers,
a knottiness of horns in which the sun
quivered like a scarlet cymbal.
Below, the sea was a swan's back –
a ruffled plumage feathering the black.
Our skiff was beached on a humpback of stones.

A goat cropped at marram tussocks,
and under shelter of a quarry
we saw the coastguard's shack
hewn out of stone, its window hit by blaze.
The sunset fumed lilac. An orange sea.

No occupant? Grass grown up in the hall,
maps pinned by rusty thumbtacks to a board
indiced with treasure-points, sunken vessels,
a Greek cargo-ship smashed on a sand-bar,
lootings from current-skeined reefs, shoals,
no evidence of any hoard
stashed in the upstairs, where a greenish star
showed through knuckles of bottle-glass.

We set up camp; our radios spoke of war
outside the world. They still couldn't locate
its radius, casualties in the East?
we'd sail with the sea-change at dawn
in search of islands risen from the sea,
uncharted, salt-licked platforms for the few
to inhabit, proclaim as new
stations this upwelling of sunken peaks,
their craggy summits steaming in the blue.

AFTER IT WAS OVER

Lopsided beeches, others had left pits
in their uprooting, gaps in a landscape
with a blue horse wintering
under an orange sun. Great knot and ring
palpable to the touch, a sunken farm,
and on the hill men shouldering

pig-trunks of wood they'll barn-stack for burning.
A century's growth gone in a night of storm,
whittled, decimated timbers.
A mail-van goes through with its headlights full.

This great upheaval with its torn craters
left us as sleep-walkers, planetary survivors
of a seismic flaw come out of the air,
taking stock of the earth as though a war
had altered things irrevocably.

Our way is different now, catastrophe
demands a new pattern, plot for the eye;
while black, querulously troublesome rooks
blow over, shouting in the azure sky.

MISTLETOE

The blues already dusking when they took
the wood road that December afternoon

with the full moon's chalky imprint,
patchy as a piebald, a scuffed ski-slope;

the earth too soft for a tractor's bite-treads,
and teams of Suffolk horses at the plough,

steaming in the cold, here working again,
just a decade from the millennium . . .

And where they went for pimpling mistletoe
was secret, climbing to forks to secure

the waxy leavings of the mistle-thrush,
leaves paired like horseshoes in the clinging bush.

And came back after dark, a bluish cold
worn as a weather sheen on icy cheeks,

dreaming of scented lips that would enquire
of the spray-cluster hung above the fire.

STANDING OFF

We stand offshore, the red keel's reflection
chases out into streamers of ribbon;
a snaking entanglement of scarlet
that lights up an underwater sunset.

Your single dive retrieved an octopus;
a rubbery toadstool-cap with cold eyes,
a wrist-flick turned its ink-mains inside out –
the suction-pads still clinging after death.

Pellucid turquoise at sea; but the calm's
illusory, the coastline denotes change –
the tension of conflict, incongruous
highrise levels pointing to how money

alters a landscape – here the symmetry
of coastal farmhouses are lost to new
operations that live up in the skies,
fiscal schemas independent of man's

concern to order his inheritance –
the little place on earth he calls a home.
On every coast a glass-faced cubism
looked out across the sea's neutrality?

We make towards a cove whose vertical
cliffs provide an unpropitious platform
for anything but seabirds. Clear water
inviting you to dive again shows fish

streamlined into a bright torpedo-head,
responsive to a collective leader.
Two blue-scaled bass preoccupy an hour,
and then the keel's answered by livid red

dramatics – a sunset firing the bay.
As children we had thought never to live
elsewhere, our permanence was here, and now
when we return we're glad to get away.

PRAYER

Lord of the stillness in the stone,
        the sun-ray imprisoned in that dark,
sustainer of our impossible agony
        at things tree-twisted, wrongly done,
and visible like names cut in gnarled bark,
upholder in our black uncertainty,
        our fear we are too much alone
in moving like a fly around the walls,
and hoping by speaking out to withstand
        the storm of madness threatening
to sever the web's last bright strand;
        illuminate the troubled mind,
the saw-teeth of the nerves, and lighten all
        who bunch themselves into a spider's ball
and flinch from light, the one poisoned by guilt,
and one who's lost the reason for his dread,
        and so it deepens; words don't fit
its unendurable substrata,
        and there's only speechlessness
when the mouth opens, and the dread
        the silence is inhabited
by someone else inside one's head;
lighten those worst hours when we can't accede
        to go on, and without respite
hurt ourselves deeper than the injury
        inflicted on others, despite
compassion granted; help extract
the sting that paralyses, and permit
        a clearer eye to see in depth
that suffocates, somewhere the pure
and unabstracted energy of light.

        II
Help me on afternoons more terrible
        than nights, to endure poverty,

the damp walls of a broken house, fused wires,
    the flash-light of anxiety
sounding its voltage like a fence
    circling a meadow's circumference,
when nothing but these small blue pills
    can deaden the intolerable
emptiness attendant on sitting still
    waiting for nothing to arrive;
but words that bring no consolation, no
    remedial amelioration,
only the poem's affirmative will
to outlive human suffering.
    Lord of the skylark's windy home,
the high blue spaces, hear this prayer
for the homeless, the mad, the lost,
    those who shake when the bottle's dead,
or walk the streets in loneliness
    searching for love that never comes,
and still enquire without redress
    of their unsanctioned deficit,
their unappeasable, involuntary
    inheritance of lucklessness, despair
at ever finding a way out
    of the maze. Enlighten by a word,
a sign, a token gentleness,
this state of numb confusion, relentless
    disparagement, and point the way
    to beginning over again
the slow ascent to light, the gradations
    of blue that come at break of day.

STARDUST

Her child's called Stardust. He's detachable
from his environment: a frequency
transmitted to his cells and he's able

to bilocate. Sometimes he'll be inside
playing with a toy robot, and she'll think
it's more instructive for him if I hide

and watch him dramatise his other life;
the one in which his face is solarised
and he's married to an astronaut wife,

and it's reality, his different speech,
his eyes changing colour from blue to gold,
the easy way in which he's learnt to reach

economy of argument; no hands
or volubility. Then he moon-walks,
his movements slow as though churning up sands

the wind has drifted on a beach. She turns
volume control and watches him re-earth,
and there's no split. The little that she learns

about his double rôle she has to keep
suspended, blueprint it in a novel
she dreams of writing. Even deep in sleep

he has an eye open, a direct ray
focused on something that he won't let go
and shines clear as a diamond in the day.

AFTER THE GREAT DISCOVERIES

After the great discoveries the maps
were altered, what was land was sea,
and what was sea became deserts, plateaus,
stone forests. A red bird flew in the sky
announcing changes. Where is Nebraska?
the white-suited American
released his Cadillac's shaded window,
and we indicated back somewhere, anywhere
across a savanna to the ocean.
Coral trees with seashells for fruits
were incongruous visuals on the road
that led to the expatriate café –
a resurrected Dallas hall,
a singer smooching over a piano,
improvising without a memory.
The patrons talked of Nisir, Ararat,
the lost sanctuaries, mountains under sea,
and of reversion, things stood upside down
might rectify. It's all illusory…

Outside the air was so intensely blue
it powdered the road with crystals. We drove
in no direction. In the displacement,
sharks, whales, dolphins had died stranded and showed
as roadside monuments. We drove to keep
ourselves from entering a sleep
in which we hallucinated. Times Square
was sapphire; fish flickered through the subway.
We tuned in to our radio
and heard Sinatra singing from some town
they were still building, 'Hey sunshine,
the blue blue water keeps on coming down.'

MADONNA

It's all a question of identity,
someone is lost inside the mutations,
the years which happen fast, schematically,
the boy-toy cat in jeans and cap

growing to be a Monroe look-alike,
blonde hair falling as though blown by the wind
emphasising whatever facial plane
is explored from behind a mike

or angled for the lens, paparazzi
hassling for every off-mood shot –
the smudged lipstick or baggy overcoat,
the private person eating green pasta

in a small restaurant, feeling for space
after the provocation, topless thrust,
the body a sequined snakeskin
transmitting white heat, an electric lust

wired to the music. And behind the face
is the new one awaiting invention;
Madonna in orange velvet leggings
dropping popcorn nuggets into her bra

at business meetings and retrieving them,
her tongue a corolla between red lips.
It's the emptiness of being a star,
the dehumanised ennui has her change

persona, image. She would like to be
both sexes: gay-male's her alter-ego,
experience every kind of orgasm;
but now, just stares out at the New York snow

from a dark blue couch, relaxes her curves
after the gym work-out, the jacuzzi,
and wishes she was a snowballing child
whacking impacted ice at a dumb tree.

DUSTING THE ARM-REST

Poetry is a wolf watching the world,
feral dog-eyes yellowing in the night,
coming at things from wild interiors,
uncompromising where it kills;

always a ranging outsider.
A child, a wolf came to me in a dream
and made to leap. The hands I raised
to ward it off were written on with words.

Poetry sleeps too often, tries to beg
acceptance with the complacent.
It's closer to the street-corner, the edge,
the solitary who arrive without precedent –

Blake, Rimbaud, the distraught Artaud,
the hallucinated, the criminal,
the one standing with his back to the wall,
defiant, while the rain blows in.

The wolf is restless, drops down from the hills
to browse amongst parked cars. It's everywhere;
its bolt announcing change, smashing a hole
through ideologies, leaving its mark

on the blue day. A winter's night, a moon
pointing a glacial brushstroke.
There's revolution in the agonised
twisting of a shriek into words.

Lean, angry, unshakeably polarised,
the night-intruder's there to hit its mark,
imparting a savage dementia
to the one waiting for it in the dark.

KEEPERS OF THE NIGHT

I bring them stories to propitiate
their watchful eyes. And we are so many
who take our allegories to a place
heaped with dead birds and multi-national flags,
a burnt piano, the life-size mannequins
of tyrants, dictators, universal
agents of ruin. Smoke drifts into space
above that threshold, and the keepers stay
like guards we never see. We know they're there,
and still demand we bring the old story
of life and loss to them; the warped spiral
of all our inconsistencies, the thread
that snaps while we approve its right tension,
the things that happen and seem without cause,
but alter us. They're not indifferent:

they seem to say the clue is in the tale,
but we can't find it or have forgotten
the meaning. We've left it to drown
like a white horse trapped in a quarry pool;
we thought it was an hour ago
it went missing, but it is years. The days
are like that, stabilising round the night
when we elucidate the happenings
that take us to the edge of a city
so many wars have passed through. It is dark:
I've made the journey in a century
that's part of time. White ashes dust the air.
I hear a voice say, 'tell me if you dare…'

DETOXIFICATION

So help me purify,
whatever new cells will regenerate
my clean blood at the end of it,
the cellular need no longer this desperate
fight in the dark hours to get free
of the cycle's remorseless continuity,
the chemical's biography
controlling mine. We're a duality,
old partners in this game of high and low
and more latterly
as cross-currents in a whirlpool.

The pain's inhuman. When I breathe
sand pours into my mouth, my nerves are stretched
along the white line of a road
over which humming cars explode
in red flashes. I've lost a skin,
an onion peeled to the interior,
and things move in –
faces that threaten, voices amplified,
an army kicking through a shell-gapped house.

I break my trust and recourse to the drug,
promising it's the final one
before I kick the habit, and succumb
to quiet, the torn skin knits back,
and faithfully ascendant, it rises,
my black inner chemical sun.

JAYS

The sky opens in the wing's feathering –
an azure rift accordioned into black
and white as the pinions disclose.

The idea of the bird in mental space:
it was blue all over,
vulnerably bright, then chestnut and rose
above me with its survivor's primal
communicative urgency
lifted from carbonised forests.

I stood confused by the nature of reality:
the air like silk on my face,
the jay in another dimension, fixed

into codified instincts, his world more than mine,
with my inner retreat, my imagining
him as he is or not.
Autumn around; leaf-gold and rot.

I walked on with the real bird in my head,
jet eyes alert, head tilted forward, wings
fanned; agonised gutturals;

and left my imaginary jay in depleted
oak-leaves; a turquoise outsider,
eyes full of journeys, forests, extinguished planets,

conceiving how he'd alter the nature of things
through the exchange of inner and outer,
dreaming the world and finding both still there,

the lifted visual, the claw's grip on bark.

GRAFFITI ARTIST

The red graffiti sprayed across a wall
in Sanskrit ciphers is my clue today
to something obvious that's drifted wide
of meaning. Written up to stay,
the air-brush calligraphist's left a skull
dead centre to his cryptic diagram;
and at the street corner a red arrow
points upwards to the sky. He left that way,
or so I like to think or disappeared
into the night with his fragmented text
punctuating his journey through alleys,
one startling visual leading to the next
and non-sequential: each a found poem

that lives like segments of a chopped up snake.
What is his language? It's intentional
and recognisably linked to our own;
a sort of latter day prophetic script
that works like a director's speeded take,
jolting the senses to a colour flash,
a violent red, green or fluorescent pink.
I could follow his trail, pick through the trash
for his individual cut-ups and read
a future in his day-glo dialect,
and perhaps in time complete the story
he's left open-ended.
                              Imagine it,
meeting him in the process of his art,
a parking lot at 2 a.m.: concealed,
not wishing to intrude, watching his hand
engaged in a vocabulary, his line
hurried, embellished: a cap on his head,
and on his denim back, a purple heart.

GEORGE
for Alan

Generous man, exuberant with life,
your big hands carrying Jamaican warmth,
you come back busy in my memory
as my eye turns on colours at this stall,
pineapple, mango, avocado, peach,
exotic fruits that I associate with you
by temperament. We knew your buoyancy,
your spontaneity, and how you lived
for simple things, the pulsing reggae beat
or pop that sounded from your room.
A tear snakes right across my memory,
smelling these fruits and knowing you won't taste
their scent again. That last time in the hall
with Alan, how could I know it for that,
a valediction: you on a spiral
of such agonisingly speeded-up decline,
there wasn't time to ever talk again,
you living out your last weeks, unconscious;
no word could get through. Now a beady rain

delays me at this street market. I think
of your obsessive array of colognes
and how I read their names, and of the clothes
you loved, stylish, flamboyant as the dahlias
you cultivated: red, yellow and white,
spiky crowns, little sea-anemones.
Displaced in London, you carried the sun
inside you, waiting only to return
to islands. And your gift was love;
the one that's missed by he who shared your life
and waits to know if you're alright. You are.
We sense that. Generosity translates
into the spirit. Now the rain gives off.
The glaze around me lights up like a star.

ARSONIST

Derelict. He slept in basements,
cocooned in paper; his black suit
concertinaed, his face bricky, raw,
hedgehogged with silver stubble.

Dust was his irritant, caked hands
he longed to cool in the river
he'd fly-fished in childhood
feeling his mauve fly shiver

the eddies. If it was a smell, a light
communicated to him as a source
of estrangement, it was the rage
repressed as fire that made it worse.

He'd got to know interiors,
night watchmen, and the image of a fox
bolting from the first blaze he'd lit
in furze, remained indelibly russet.

The pressure building in dry heat,
he knew it had to be out, something burn
other than his disordered nerves.
He hallucinated flames at his feet

and shrank from policemen, passersby.
That day he kept in a warehouse,
knowing he'd do it, there was gasoline
and turpentine left by painters,

rats and a dead one jewelled by flies.
The rear gave on to an apartment block.
He came out at night hypnotised
by his inner vision; the shock

would jolt him back into reality,
watching among the crowds the roaring crack
of flames fissure a building, turning round,
calm, with the fire reflected on his back.

LETTERS

A surf of rectangles. I'm always late
to prune the jumble, the panopticons
of a disordered spate;
a cataract that's left to spill.

Sometimes they're like square snow-prints on table
and floor, and variegated, black and pink
or red and blue, a mosaic
frescoed with stamps, blank-ink

medallions. The ones I recognise,
the ones I don't and open cautiously
for the wasp or the butterfly
unfolding from the page.

Fifteen a day. A global avalanche;
a dependably reassuring fall.
They crackle in my hands, wallets, sachets,
a paper artichoke I unpetal

to reach the heart.
And each so individual
in ways that letters admit more than speech,
are orchestrated by mood and personal

obsessions, leitmotivs, and if we met
we'd find each other different,
shrugging those issues, making light
of what goes deep; the stone in the dark core.

I fish the pile and forget none;
it's like the childhood game in which
I didn't look and with a magnet on a string
retrieved topheavy cardboard carp

from an aquarium. I test the feel.
We're lifelines to each other; paper birds
launched on impossible trajectories.
We leave our flight-runs; little scores of words . . .

TOAD

The one I rescued from a cat: so small
it seemed a nimble brooch cupped in my hands,
a coolness imparted to warmth,
immobile, unprotesting, flippery,
I carried it back from that lit alley
one hot night in July, dry, thundery,
the air stubbornly ungiving, a match
and the heath would crackle, jump with red flame.

You followed as I nursed our red-eyed captive,
skin mottled like army dungarees,
a yellow pebbling on the sage-green skin
with buffs and earth-browns pigmented
by way of camouflage. How could it know
my intentions, this rapid conveyance;
a warm pulse thudding at its cool?

We placed it undercover
in a dark corner; and fat spots of rain
arrived in answer to a sympathy
coextensible between us and it,
the two month drought terminated, the shower
torrential, steamy, bubbling into cracks.
We came alive after the walled heat,

and thought of our domestic talisman,
little chthonic household god,
provident with blessings, and this perhaps
the first of many prompted felicities?
We flung the windows wide on the night rain,

its silver sluicing through the dense lime trees.

CLEARANCE

Red sunlight picks out letters in the wall;
the crudely hatched interlacing of names
united at that moment in a heart
scratched into granite: Summer '69

Joanna/Dave: the inscription reads still
above the tide-line, compacted glitter
schisted in stone, each wink a mineral.
Their lives and mine? the intersection cuts

obliquely, for I've known this beach
as a sounding-board to each emotion
picked out since childhood; clearance, confusion,
the wave's sky-window lifting to the chin,

concussive fear, the arms striking to reach
a handhold in the surf, the smashed sapphire
running for shore … This early evening calm
sets up a contemplative air,

beer-cans, used tubes of Ambre Solaire –
the afternoon's debris awaits the surf,
a random montage pointing. We were here
and left an unconscious exhibit

to comment for us, should we disappear;
and Joanna and Dave, where they are now,
together or apart is speculative,
their names linked in the impulse to survive

a summer's incandescence, keep intact
whatever they knew then and realised
as burning and could qualify
by writing up the inconclusive fact.

DE SADE

A grey dress coat, deep orange silk breeches,
a feather in his hat, he's thirty-two.
The château of Lacoste is pure gothic.
He wants to socialise aberration,

and have a spiked whip cut her black and blue;
he only ever enters from behind;
a woman's pubis doesn't interest him.
He cuts his flagellant's score into wood

with a sharp knife. Erotomania
will have him savage man or woman, force
his overreach to a dementia
he can't modulate. He finds the body

lacks sufficient points of entry,
he would give it a new geometry
to satisfy his frustration.
After the act there's nothing left to do

but dissociate, work it out again.
At fifty-three his body's new ballast
in prison affords him a pig's belly.
His hair is sand-white, his black coat is torn,

he squats like a toad in his cell
and threatens to expand from wall to wall.
He's found a more protean irritant,
the revisioning of sex word by word,

each close-up magnified by abstention,
for now there's greater elasticity
in the perverse co-ordinates achieved
through the contortions of anatomy…

His back supported the Bastille
as a granite turtle-shell. Raging blood.
Free, he ordered baskets of red roses,
sniffed each and trampled them into the mud.

THE CATCH IN THE STAIRS

It caught us out, the unexpected gap
in a deserted lighthouse; its rusty spiral stair
severed, stove in by boulder-heads
that vandals brought to it. Half up, half down,
our momentum returned on itself
as though our minds had gone up to the top
and blindingly returned. Hoarse gulls somewhere,
and further out a swagging blue-green sea.
We climbed backwards into the tilting light,
recalling other stairs, marble, granite,
treacherous, rimed sills leading from a wharf
one night in Venice, the vaporetto
audibly bisecting canals. Distance
created by that sound. And others too;
your leading me up a vertical flight
in a tight skirt to an attic studio,
and coming down barefoot, afraid to fall.
We've found our balance on so many gradients,
one foot forward, one back, or suspended
between decisions, meeting up again
to find a level in the sunlit hall.

BETWEEN THE 3ᴿᴰ AND 5ᵀᴴ

Our meeting came by accident,
exchange of eye-beams and improvident
to immediate fulfilment. "Two years',
you said, 'and meet me on a bridge
above the river, the 3ʳᵈ and 5ᵗʰ, and I'll be there
awaiting you.' I watched you disappear
out of the café door, black hair, red coat,
a Japanese face, small red mouth,
but tall and leaving on the air
an unidentifiable perfume.

I lived with your image in mental space
and tried to draw your resistant features
imagining you jetsetting from place to place
or looking over a lover's shoulder
into our projected future,
the lamps on bridges all over Europe
clearing the bluish haze, a white ferry
lit up as a restaurant,
my returning at hourly intervals
with eyes searching the face of each stranger,
apprehensive, prepared to stay. 'I'm here
between the 3ʳᵈ and 5ᵗʰ. I walked out
on my life for you; the black river
couldn't care less. In my country
the harvest is one of abundant grapes.
I've written you into a book. I fear…'

And now the summer's burnished. I prepare
in my mind for your arrival,
stone lions watching, a blue in the light
picking out red and gold, finding your hair's
divide at the crown – will it be like that
tied up, wind-blown, a black coat not a red
hurrying through the capital
before the last swallow, the early night.

UNDERCURRENTS

1
They converse in the stairwell. It is late.
He might have blown the other, zipped him up,
and now the altercation, the flawed date,

the impresario's tamed falsetto,
the grab at leather under a nursed light,
muted recriminations. One must go

after the risk, the bolting of a door,
back into the night: red and green twinklings
lighting the port, and up on the fourth floor

a lamp extinguished. The small incident
carries, is transmitted to other minds
who build a narrative from the event,

diversifying context. Was it that?
a pick-up who was desperate, a blood-spot;
the hunted one now downstairs in his flat?

2
The issue's always unresolved.
He's married and walks back through streets.
His life is like a bookmark in the night's
open fiction, a red braid showing dawn
above the harbours. It's the undertow
threatens, the altogether blacker pool
in which his emotions feed.
                            Now he stands,
resting against the sea-wall. Heavy surf
breaks on this side, a fomenting dazzle
pushing a stone necklace across the sand.

3
The dream-book's written and we're all in it,
only we'll never live to reach its end
or know where it begins. Others live us,
extending possibilities
to how the action's never localised,
but diversified into the story.

It happened once, but these are variants –
the slow-exposure flash revealed a face
preoccupied by inner space;
the images connecting with a page
we'll never read. It's turned over each night
by the archival myth that rules the stars,

and we wrote it, the continuity.

THE UNEXPECTED LESSON

Red leaves in my hands. The world is harder now;
the ladder I let fall so long ago
has rotted under straw, the open roof
admitted smoking rains, the raging equinox.

White horses of rain streaming through dark woods.
Today the little boy and little girl
he invented as a solitary friend
have taken shelter in my broken moods

and look out from a flawed highrise city
at detonative traffic, red plane trees,
and I remember a white handkerchief
with blue initials in the boy's pocket,

a square of mist or a blindfold
to keep me from things that I wouldn't see,
parental discord, a bird on the road
still shivering from an open red wound;

how was it possible that things should die?
How is it possible that they still do?
I'm still no nearer a resolution,
each year sees the foot try a thinner crust

above the seismic flaw. And nights are bad.
I find myself lost in a dream city,
the crowds stand pointing up at my parents
who kneel on a rooftop divided by

a dead flamingo fallen at their feet.
A jewel leaks from its eye. It seems to know.
Red leaves in my hands. The skies are flying low.
I break words open on a concrete street.

ARCHIVAL

When we came back after the first time away
the earth had changed. We heard of ruins held
captive by the new military,
a diamond monolith raised from carbon;
a blonde woman who drove round in a car
all night, stopping to aerosol digits
on sites for potential landings.
But no one came after us to relieve

our shock, our disorientation;
the red dust glare that smudged the horizon.
We found a group of black matchstick children
conducting a judicial trial
over a dead US pilot.
Whatever the verdict he'd have no burial.
After we left they lit a fire.
Birds we had never seen before
flew over, big armour-plated grey birds
that might a century ago
have been our aircraft, bound for the desert.

In a building turned upside-down
I sifted through a bank's archives.
Wills, assets, vault deposits, names, the names
with which we'd once identified,
and just one suspect oddity – Skyray –
an interplanetary spy?
The blonde woman? We'd never know,

already we were building beneath a red sky.

THE NEW AGE

We're in it, and it's caught us unawares;
the take-over was a premonition
that grew to a reality, a cloud-shadow
that never forecasted the sparkling shower
and how its silver bites back from the road.
How can I direct poetry
towards the future's disconnected images
that flash by on a filmic screen?
The word's gone underground. I heard it go
into the night guided by a gold star.
The swallows search for it, frisking the air
at dusk above this violet square.

The visual qualities pronounce themselves;
the superficial's surface-excess wins
by hooking our sensory need; that car,
that girl in leather with mauve sunglasses
are interchangeable with the movie
we've come out from, the stage-set is the same,
and music lifts us to a roof-garden;
the sequined guests look up as a helicopter
monitors the traffic canyons.
We're all in each other's film and conscious of that,
live through the imitative and not the real.
My words are a headless stem on a page;
I'm distracted by a red hat,
slashed jeans, a gold shoe, solarised faces,
the whole coloured accoutrement the poem wears
stepping into the imponderable age.

HEY

An end of it. Meeting like this.
It's an infraction on society
the things we do in public. You and I.
A red cherry trapped inside a crystal,
so the winter sunset seems,
an ideogram, a haiku, scarlet
efflorescence in a cone.

This way not that is what we know.
The risk, the meeting out of time,
your Paisley tie unmasted, vulnerable
to whatever the threat we undergo –
your wife, executive infrastructure.

We lose the hour; a dead moth hangs
its folded parachute in the window.

BLACK SUGAR

Or call her the enigma. What she stole
or where she hid was a chiaroscuro
of worked-out guesses. She was singing soul

in a night-spot in hardly anything
under a focused spotlight when we met;
her hand loaded with sparkles, one blue ring

a diamond planet liquid with her wrist.
A girl thief who drove a pink truck,
her double actions emphasised the twist

that had her steal. When she was up on-stage
her character was unified; she lived
inside the song and not the spiral rage

that took her out to dark places alone,
or up to unlit apartments, her hands
wanting to do the things her mind had done,

anticipating this. There was a need
involved in her selection, a speed-flash
that thrilled her nerves, and a spontaneous greed

to loot and go. She got caught with the Ming
china, the owner came back, found her there,
and all that she could think to do was sing.

TRANSVESTITES

We live the gender split as cross-overs
to an assumed identity. A game,
a risk, we're mostly volatile lovers

excited by transference; look, a twist
of silk around my neck, a lipstick gash,
a tinted foundation and I exist

as more alive, more consciously as me
than any other rôle I might adopt.
A public challenge? It's temerity

that's needed to confront the street; I try
to make it natural; red and black and white,
a pencil line drawn round each almond eye;

I am my own artistic creation,
I find the face I want to wear, select
my brushes for each primed situation

and meet it like that. It's unnatural
to be so recognisably the same;
most men will never know the ritual

that goes with making up. The risk is there,
also the joy of finding in strangers
a welcoming vindication, a stare

that's followed by a girl's smile, and we meet,
both brightly coloured, talking in the wind
that blows cherry blossoms across the street.

ELVIS PRESLEY

He's photographed against a Cadillac,
one of the many littering his park,
white shoes conspicuous against the black

jacket, the cliff edges around the quiff
broken by gelled strands, loose diagonals.
His posture's always informally stiff,

it seems to say, 'I am the first and last
to make music into a religion.
My virtue is in owning to no past,

and yet the present leaves me obsolete.'
The antebellum façade at Graceland
has two stone lions guarding the retreat;

the rooms are kitsch, an ersatz movie set,
no sound, no light, and yet the *mise-en-scène*
describes the man: wall-to-wall mirrors vet

the ostentation without commentary.
A red room, blue room, chandeliers, peacocks,
each piece has no familiarity,

but suggests someone filling in a space
eclectically, obsessed by the unreal,
catching sight of himself in a surface

in which a sculpture preens. His fall was long,
cushioned by chemical supernovas.
We listen. Who is that inside the song?

MARC BOLAN

So diminutive even up on heels,
his eyes are two black craters; he commits
the lyric to an understated drawl,
a moody venom injected with hints

that it's not all an act, and the guitar
pursues descending phrases, solo licks
that vitalise a time peculiar
to his predominance, a glam guru

statuette-sized as Wagner or Lautrec
in a rain-storm of sequins. He is mean
in ways the audience demand,
untouchable, withdrawn beneath rucked hair,

a style, a genre without a precedent,
and soon used up, burnt out current,
no visible transition, one foot snared
in past successes, one without a hold

on shifting, earthquake ground, a silver boot…
The myth's to die incomplete, unfulfilled,
and sometimes it proves a reality,
a miscalculation behind the wheel,

the car's tin can concertina,
all aspirations left illusory,
uncontactable, sirens everywhere,
a crow taking off to a nearby tree.

ROCK AND POETRY

One feeds the other. It's the subversive
I value – speed injected into words,
the volatile flash lifting syllables
into a rain forest of coloured birds,

a storm of scarlet, green and gold.
Poetry needs street-cred, an energy
vital to youth; two standing out the rain
in Greek Street, reading their own memory

of now and what it means to be alive
in someone else's words. *He* got it right,
rain moving in and out of a blue cloud ridge
makes brilliant statements about the light,

accents the April day and tinctures it
like the black corolla inside a flower.
And there's another way to make it live;
her Walkman starts to crackle with the power

of menacing feedback: a voice cuts in
that's separated by the mix; it too
speaks of an up day through a minimal
novella; a red car pursues a blue,

the girl smiling at the boy at the lights,
then slipping away into dense traffic
is lost for ever, an elusive blonde
he thinks of in his solitary attic,

and the guitars chase her all over town…
It's a dynamic: rock and poetry
meeting in individual ways
to make sense of our age, of you and me

welcoming each liberative gesture
that gets us nearer cutting the ribbon
on impositions, living to the full
and celebrating how that freedom's won.

LOVING THAT MAN OF MINE

The timing's flawless. When she meets the phrase
it's like a line considered by the heart
so long it colours phrasing. Mauve to blue.

Bringing it out and turning notes is like
biting into an orange by the sea
and testing loneliness. He never cares
or will according to her need,
the fur coat, perfumes, hardly mean a thing
to a torch singer spotlit at the mike
bleeding the texture of a song.

And song's about the flaw we never mend,
the inequalities in love,
the mistimings, seeing him walk away
into the big unknown one rainy night.

She won't go offstage any happier,
but for a moment somatises loss,
head cradled in one hand, the other up,
a brooch catching fire at the throat
and when the song cuts she's still travelling
the deep hurts back to an expiring note.

THE COLONEL'S MACHINATIONS

The blindside man. Rumbustious,
ex-fairground, entrepreneurial whizz,
cigar-stoppered bark, bellicose
PR belligerent hit-bulk
of Elvis management.
Stipulator of non-negotiable
winner-takes-all contractual rights,
his scrunched fedora's seated back
as though impacted there, green mash
of unattended felt.
He's real-lifed from a gangster film,
moon-faced crude rube, monogamous
to his creation, nowhere man,
no roots, no past, no history,
just Elvis starlit on his mind
as godspeak. Wacky in his groove
he's a jocular snow dealer,
a paunchy lumbering bison
kneeling on violets where they grow,
his whiphand always undertoned.
His ways clear forests at a swipe,
old huckster dug up from the South
to network for the blinding new
with mock affection for hot property
and quizzed amusement at his sell.
The incongruities marry,
the seasoned and naïve death-trip
towards a Hollywood gold bowl
lined with blue diamonds. He's admonitory,
keeps Elvis islanded inside Graceland,
non-contributive to biography…
His hold's a strangulating python's grip,
a breath-squeezed-out paralysis.
Elvis gets flattened, damp-mooded,
dispirited and learns by rote
a silent acquiescence, dubs his will

to Thom's despotically crash oversee,
his threats track-listed from a gun
concealed inside his mind, the safety catch
half on, half off, the sights lensed on EP.

THE SIXTIES

A tidal wave slams thunder on the beach,
the violent uproar in its undertow
communicated as shock frequencies
to bikers sitting out along the road...

Changes dance in a marijuana haze,
an acrid weed-fog feeds defiant youth.
They come together on a loaded vine
at Woodstock, Monterey, the Isle of Wight,

all beads and boots, the men dressed Regency,
his shirt surfing with frill-stacked lace,
her mini, a pink satin afterthought
to being naked. Now it's 'Purple Haze'

freak-storms the airwaves with its driving riffs;
the drugs turn visionary, a microdot
activates all the glowering archetypes.
Lee Harvey Oswald sights a temple vein

big as a power line and blows Kennedy
into death's silent auditorium.
Everywhere insurrection. Monroe dead,
her blonde hair blowing through infinity...

The King stays underground, shored up on pills
to numb his isolation, clouded fame.
He sleeps all day. His rivals strut the boards
windstormed by overloaded decibels,

 an insolently hip Mick Jagger preens
into a sea of lookalikes, one hand
controlling thirty thousand devotees.
Somebody high on acid, starts to pray...

Elvis retreats into his king-size bed,
resentful of a marriage he would smash.
Priscilla blue-rooms mornings on her own,
the fuse-blown decade building to its crash.

JUNK-FOOD JUNKIE

The man's a cheeseburger mausoleum,
an appetent contortionist
snake-bloated on cholesterol junk,

intestinal-roomy as a silo
housing a grain harvest: he'll eat his way
through bear-sized stacks of burgers and French fries,

a deconstructing monument
of sinuous bacon-eddies in fat.
Heroic eating in the present tense,

no grammar to his bite, he gristles all
unpalatably hexed inedibles
into a stomach-vault for safe-keeping,

a colonic labyrinth to a tomb
of decomposing treasure. Elvis eats
proportionate to fame and limo-size

mashed potatoes, pork chops, cornbread, compact
ice creams big as Jayne Mansfield's tits,
kitchen-cut peanut butter quadrangles,

tyre-size Spanish omelettes, a butter rinse
on everything, a greasy slick.
He chews for three: dead mother and dead twin

are fibred in his chicken. He lies back:
his dead are happy and crème caramel
stays on his taste buds like the scent of fern.

DIVORCE

Contracted blood money. He'd kill Mike Stone,
the wounded King's decree is spit and shoot
as volatile appeasement of his pain.
The telephone's a ripped-out liana.
He spraycans Day-Glo threats across the wall

and rages at her infidelity,
the girl he's cheated on from a perverse
miscalculated sense of loyalty –
he keeps her as the inviolable one,
and feeds his kicks on coming back to her

in brutally duplicitous penance.
She's gone, and freedom hurts without restraint.
His threats obscenely free associate,
Priscilla's shacked in Pacific Palisades
duetting with her karate icon,

while Elvis snake-bloats on triple French fries
and mind-schemes homicidal bloodlettings.
At night, he shifts from floodlit room to room
obsessed she's there in hiding, white on white,
contritely naked in a tiara...

His wounded machismo finds no respite
in vindicatory back-up from the boys.
A sapphire earring's underlit night sky,
a rack of frosty silks, marabou pumps,
are a reminder trail like face powder

still granulated on a red cushion
of her inflammable need to want out.
He bumps into his guilt and runs away
as though a forest fire made savage tracks
and singed his hammered break towards the road...

His past is torn along a jagged seam.
He'll substitute dumb bimbos for his doll,
grow bitter from betrayal, recluse himself
inside a Bible, looking for a love
that burns so bright it's unconditional.

LOOKING OUT (LOOKING AT YOU)

One in 12 million in the London grid,
a passing fact, an info-
kit of unshareable biography –
age 25? nationality
Hispanic? blood type O? hair hennaed red?
shoe size a 4? dress size a 10
for emphasis? favourite non-colour black?
coffee place Starbucks? and romantically
resourceful to my eye-bite questionnaire
Nietzsche's Zarathustra topping
a hobbled, crushed black velveteen
girlie-secret (Miss Selfridge?) shoulder bag,
the Nietzsche feeding me subjectively
the cross-link to a shared vision?
                         We share this space
inside a Prêt à Manger on Frith Street,
her blue nail polish (Bourjois?) eyeliner
a cobalt (No. 17?), black jeans
label hidden, a sassy (D&G?),
grey cashmere jumper (Jigsaw?), black bra-strap
a pointy (Gossard Wonderbra?)
big-screen sunglasses (Boots or a Drugstore?)
shelved like a filmstar's in her hair:

we simultaneously perched looking out
on the October day, the light so gold
it's like chilled Chablis in its clarity.
She makes to go, a little part of me
in her awareness? and looks back
inviting me to apprehend the loss?
a once seen undateably neat stranger
busy about her life, (Anna?) (Alex?)
gone on to (Borders?), (HMV?),
while I deliberate the possibilities
we'll meet again like characters
inside a real time fiction, and pass by
rainily conscious of what might have been
love at first sight without the need to try.

PENGUIN MODERN CLASSICS

My first 1960s spine-damaged casualties,
grey vertebrae so fingerstopped
they're strafed like split bamboo,

still present a flaky grey fortress wall
of biffed-in European indie-cult
landsliding from a saggy shelf.

Generic pointers to hip-lit,
I deepened reading Kafka, Camus, Sartre,
tripped East with Hermann Hesse, back West

to Thomas Mann's filigree aesthetic,
learnt from Genet that evil preens
its shadow-aspects like a maroon rose.

Gide was a recherché apéritif
to pointillistic Pasternak.
I read my way through Europe, by the sea.

Decades later the logo's revamp binds
old building blocks and new.
Greene's *Brighton Rock*'s the offbeat prototype

to Burroughs's *Junky*; Kerouac turbos
hot pace across a continent.
Paul Bowles packs crushed ice into metaphor

maintaining prose at zero-cool.
Nabokov's *Lolita* re-sells
its disingenuous ingenue

to the autumnal libido…
I give my climacteric shelf
its necessary H.R.T.,

buy in a stack, and walk them home beneath
a sky so bluish-green I'm young again
reading the summer out on a white beach.

THE FUTURES

They patented the name: Jacky and Jack,
a same-sex tango; burial their theme
in all its glitzy posthuman flavours.

The queens they buried in faux leopardskin.
One had his ashes mixed with pink sequins,
then dusted from a chartered plane

over an iffy cruising park.
One had a heart-shaped lightbox coffin done
so friends could see to the interior.

Once on a strafish, leaf-stripped, slippery day
ambered by shifty light, they took requests
for customised from James, a diced body

canned in his favourite catfood tins,
the artefact kept permanent inside
a glass display twinkly with fairy-lights.

Kevin was adamant: chocolates inside,
and dark Swiss chocolate covering the box
to offer sugar hits for mourners.

One was to be buried in a pink fridge,
another in a Cadillac,
the little details articulated –

toenails and fingernails glossed black.
One asked for burial on the moon
he was so inveterately solitary.

The firm upgraded, they prospected their deaths
as absolute togetherness,
both to be converted into Smarties

and consumed by a mutual friend,
Jacky as pink and orange, Jack as brown
and lilac, with the rest as lucky chance.

LAPSANG SOUCHONG

A China black.
A tarry king-leaf's morbid tang,
it smells October, woody notes

bonfirish to selective taste,
or sometimes it's dead hyacinths,
wet hemp, or a port's soupy pool

whiff in as undertow-analogies
to Lapsang's sensory ensemble,
its medley of wisteria

and bacon café-fried at 9 a.m.
An emperor saw the tea flavoured by rope
and sipped it inspirationally,

took a chest north, savoured keemun,
orchid and oolong, kept his choice
as companion to writing poetry.

My chunky, cube-faced Fortnum's tin
is spooned each day, vampy tannins
and caramelised sugars

feeding my toxin-quota, imparting
a furred cuff to the tongue.
The fat leaves bloat

like tadpoles in the cooling pot.
A ritual sourced by a habit,
I win the tea's distinctions, cup by cup,

the first a smoky amber brew,
the second muddier, the last
deep river churning with autumnal rot.

ELEGY FOR DAVID GASCOYNE

Three streets away from where I write,
plane leaves wallpaper Tanza Rd.,
their floppy, star-shaped autumn mush
mashed orange round your old front door –
your 1930s sanctuary,
a base from which to walk all night

across the city's meshed network,
its bridges and financial grid
appearing almost visionary:
you hungry, drugged, and looking out
for the dawn's first Campari blast
to colour red over Southwark.

Your walks to me are legendary,
deep night a complicitous state
to constellating metaphor:
the poem memorised as hot,
then worked on by those molecules
which are its individual chemistry.

Bartók and Berg were your thrashed mix
of soundscape geometries, hit hard
into your fine-tuned, shot-down nerves.
You rose at noon, wore pin-stripe suits,
a studied tie, saw London burn
in a heat-flashed, war-time apocalypse.

So often, David, I still meet
your benefactor from the time;
her speedwell-blue eyes, blue like yours,
with recollection, while we talk
through leaf-fall, with its mosaic
mottling the toad-spotted wet street.

Today, with sunlight bottled into haze
like colour in an ice-lolly,
I stand on Kite Hill and map out
the city's rudiments – your beat –
a gold star on Canary Wharf
sighting above the compact maze.

My memories of you are late,
your 1980s rediscovery;
we sharing readings, you benign
and anecdotal, telling me Breton
wrote in green ink, Crevel violet,
with total recall at the Tate.

You checked your watch compulsively
for an appointment neither made
nor kept, a secret rendezvous
with time itself, outside de Chirico's
station, framed by a dark green sky
dissolving boundaries of reality?

You gave your life to poetry,
demanding nothing, went insane
like Hölderlin, your gift burnt out,
and revisioned with dignity
the art of silence, made of it
an abstract creativity.

Poets are born to give and not receive,
the story of our damaged lives
in making out: you sold your books,
your everything, no back up then
as now, just a fraternity
attempting somehow to survive.

Breton you agreed, was the last
to raise a cosh for poetry
as revolutionary credo.
Expelled from the group, you remained,

post-ECT, its survivor,
an undercover surrealist.

Your letters, I have 63,
punctuated reclusive years,
your blanks in time, no impetus
to get back, just your memories
tuned to past highlights, like a film
in which you were the commentary.

You are a legend to the few
who know your journey, and I feel
your presence in the smoky air,
the youthful poet, red bussing
to the West End, and Zwemmer's Books,
sometime in 1942?

I write this in a small café,
you would have used at South End Green,
aware this poem's our last meeting place,
a point of contact I sustain
no matter unilaterally
throughout much of the foggy day.

You would, like me, in going back
have climbed the hill by slow degrees
and heard the Thameslink train address
the neighbourhood, and deep in thought
have pondered on the swimming leaves,
the red, the yellow and the black.

NIFTY JIM

Stood in my nerves at seventeen
unambiguously gay
red lipstick gash a give away
of outsider provenance,
a skinny, grey-flecked 54,
girlie jumper, slouched beret,
frenchifying genderbent
aspirations to be Dietrich.
Faced him, the lipstick hitting in,
first man I'd seen in public dare
common outrage in our town's
small-screen provinciality,
his leather shoulder-bag spilling
kleptomaniacal hoards,
indiscriminate fistfuls –
makeup, lighters, paperbacks,
random hits to compensate
for being solo in the day,
a window-shopping fugitive.
The sky was like a bottle fizzed,
an opalescent cloudy churn
in underlying racy blue,
the harbour complex where we stood
echoey with voice delay
bouncing round the grungy docks.
Something opened out in me,
that ordinary school afternoon,
doorwayed in complicity,
he loading me with trashy stash –
and years later learning his name,
the thin thief, Nifty Jim, detained
for kleptomania, I read headlined –
man in red lipstick stole for kicks.

RE-READING SYLVIA PLATH

I don't do literature, but Plath
whacking her fast ball imagery
on speed-trajectories kicks hard

and biffy on the way I read
her plugged-in dare-all energies.
December outside, and a spotty shower

teases the obdurate campanula's
wall-straggly resistant mauve flowers
holding on to the London day.

Plath's metaphors take apple-shine
on contact with the eye, and bleed
their tulip colours into violent give.

First time I read her on a beach
sand in my sightings grainily
dusting her wound on every page,

the English Channel swimming in,
metal pollutants in the undertow,
I felt her enter like a pathogen.

She's no-concessions volatile,
the poem as performing band
lays a tight rhythm on her voice.

Her trademark bite's like needle tracks
scored in 1962,
there on retrievable update,

worded to keep arriving clean
from flying without overhaul.
Sister Sylvia's fuming still

inside my consciousness, while rain comes on
as easy nothing, and campanulas
take it on floppy star-shaped crowns.

TALKIN' 'BOUT REGENERATION

The future's coloured like churned urban clouds,
sandy-grey floaters Kurt associates
with airports, beaches shelved towards the sky,

a genetically based longevity…
He's post-death recuperative. Second time.
Growth factor from a tissue engineer

had cells migrate to a spongy liver.
Death as he knows it feels like video,
his mind playing back compact footage,

a decade of acute scenarios.
He fears using up his regressive text,
the black-out total, nothing on recall.

He sits with Marilyn who's never died.
Her one repair involved nanomachines
carried around in her on tiny trains.

She thinks the sky looks wider. Potatoes
turned from her lot are earthier
this year, despite the knobbly twirls.

Kurt's on-line SNP chip selects drugs
designed for his cirrhotic trek.
She feeds him detox: a liquid sunrise

glassed-up as raunchy carrot juice.
The view's like a film-shoot. A veteran plane
hangs over on commemorative display,

then rumbles altitude at roof level.
He knows the process will keep happening,
death as it's dealt in multiples.

The aircraft's colours are like combat gear.
Kurt feels time moving on his skin
like goosebumps pointing up a chilled alert.

PEONIES

Biohazardous leaky heat
sunblocked by us, still nurtures
carnivalistic peonies
sprung from tennis ball sized buds
to carmine extravaganzas

like a Galliano hat
ice-cream scooped with ruffles.
Thrillier than camellias
they crowd on pink appeal
lollingly ostentatious

a little undercover,
reconnecting me back
to Nash-faced Regent's Park –
my seven years there like a day
burning the wires bare,

now retrospected to stand-out
particulars: Venetian blinds
slatting the light to parallels,
a West End purchased mini-tower
of books and CDs on the floor,

Harley Street backwalled on the view,
and peonies visited summers
as lipstick colours genused there
volcanoing in the gardens
beside displaying allium.

The past's coded in my biology
as shocky flashbacks, recall stuff
that kicks in unpredictably,
the accent always on surprise,
recalling the hot rain-licked day I stroked

a face-up peony's flouncy bib,
after a diagnosis, squeezed
a petal like contacting time
as something carbonated, real,
rounds on me now like a hot flush.

DANISH PASTRY

His Dior glasses mirror close-up shrink.
The pastry's solar hub is apricot,
the reddish sweet-dip planet saved till last,

all flaky dependents tracked with a fork.
He works the little cyclops to clear view
insighting calorific stickiness.

A Jaffa-livid Suzuki's parked up.
His boyfriend's unrepentant with meringue,
tongue like a snowplough tractoring through drifts.

MARINA

Five years her red-haired chutzpah,
nasturtium, poppy,
bordeaux red,
injected upbeat tempo
into our café, like an orange slash

of colour to resistant walls:
Marina in her sprayed-on jeans,
puckishly vivacious,
singing back-up chorus to
the radio –

the top notes on 'You're Gorgeous'.
Different hairstyle every day,
girlie kiss curls or a page,
sometimes a circa Thin White Duke
gelled pointer to cabaret;

makeup done with artistry,
her 23 Croatian summers
coming up sunshine in her eyes,
Marina's sparkle finning words
I streamlined for a novel…

Without her afternoons lack flash,
pop hooks lose their strawberry tang,
cappuccino its lace cuff.
I write the afternoon away
aimed for a blue vanishing point

200 pages down the line.
Our café's like a tired retread:
the aura that she rayed out gone,
her ikebana flourishes
no longer sorting pink and red

carnations to visual alert.
She won't be back. I gave her books
I wrote around her, little things
done in her orbit, looking up
to feel her presence so alive it hurt.

COLD FOG

The year's obit is fluffy with blue stuff
poured from a smoky opalescent sky
the sunrise back of it an orange block

smudged out by particle glitter.
I frisk it on high ground – Parliament Hill:
Canary Wharf signposted through the blur

like a sighting extraterrestrial.
I tunnel clingy patterning, moonstones
atomised by my breath, a shot-glass freeze

signatured on elastic skin.
A dog's red neon collar blips with stars
chased on a long curving trajectory.

Each seam I cut through is re-sewn,
my progress sealed behind me, like I walked
interzoned from reality

towards a field that's coloured like the moon.
Lack of clear focus changes what I see
into gestaltic metaphor.

I shift my options inconclusively,
a dare-all seasons swimmer hits the pond
as a flat detonation, and I hear

his slapped engagement with black density
bend echoes through cold insulating air.
I take a soapy circuit out and back

before the city presses, read into
this vaporous scarvy vocabulary
romantic undertones, a solitary

insightfulness, the way a lyric grows
from things half realised that coming clear
are polished by degrees to clarity.

EDITH GROVE

The fungi on the walls are like blue bread,
fist-sized excrescences, crop-circle whorls,
paisley blotches abseiling to the bed.

Mick's gone off with a satchel bricked with books,
the two guitarists strum with cold fingers
to old guttural Muddy Waters hooks.

They poncho blankets. A red winter sun
squeezes an orange over Chelsea docks.
Brian does slide, a riffy trick he's won.

Andrew's in town at Strickland's Record Store,
corner of Dean and Compton, riffling sounds;
the future thumps him like the subway roar.

Soho's all putzah. Johnny Danger's floor's
the third one up. A pink shirt says it all.
It signals access to fire-proofed doors.

Back in the Chelsea den, they cut it raw.
Keith's understudy Buddy Holly licks
break through the jamming like a sudden thaw.

The dishes tower like a Westway high-rise,
a scissored NME rafts on the floor,
small ads circled. Mick's make-up's a surprise –

Max Factor eye-shadows, a blue, a green
left open on the basin, Quant powder
skid-marking the rim with a dusty sheen…

Nobody loves you when you're down and out.
The heating's disconnected, room's a tip,
the mess providing the rebellious clout

to foster image – spotty bad boy loons,
defiant, dead broke, stealing guitar picks
and quickly mastering Bo Diddley tunes.

REGENT SOUND

A boxy hotel room-sized studio,
stripped ivory paint, the burnt omelette blotches
rashing the walls; a demo-space
in Denmark Street, mono only
for primitives – the Stones in there
bleeding their amps to wall of noise.

The red-haired, tie-thin Dadaist
impresario – ALO –
works the control room like a test pilot,
the accidental and the found
mixed at a level that's so raw
it detonates ear-drums.

The sounds live and direct-to-disc,
a cobbled blues-punk, teeny rip,
a sonic speedball like a Tyson fist
mashing the gobsmacked Decca head,
a spotty, in your nose, dude-bravura
breaking taboos like digging up the dead.

Jagger's a fire-eating mike-swallower
surfing his breath into the song,
needling it with subjective fangs.
They leak delay into an in-house theme,
a customised state-of-the-art motif.
Small money. Big time. An art student's dream.

Egg boxes for sound baffling, they plug in,
extemporise round an acoustic riff,
then kick a blues storm through 'Not Fade Away'.
The B-side's nailed in twenty minutes flat –
'Little by Little' with its twelve-bar blues
and churlish vocals from a lip curled cat.

They can the songs on credit, pool cab fares,
leave scuff marks from their blue Anello boots,
their moment coming, like they've grown with it
as destiny, a welling up of roots
to meet the age – they take it in their stride –
and notch up a decade of blazing hits.

CECIL BEATON PHOTOGRAPHS JAGGER

The roué's white hat sips at lilac hair,
the effete aesthete, louche Sloaney
re-tops a glass of Veuve Clicquot Grande Dame

with spirally explosive molecules
tapering to a funnelled V,
like the inclusion of a zip.

He's Englished in the level heat,
cassis silk tie like blackcurrant
ribbed across vanilla ice cream.

He thumbs a misanthropic Graham Greene,
the plot bleached like the equator
revivified by Scotch and soda,

and feels the age-gap tighten like a belt
forced on the flight at 40,000 feet.
He's run flat up against déclassé love,

like Thomas Mann's for Tadzio,
the eunuch Jagger sequenced in his brain
as a repeat chemical high,

a tight-bunned hairpin-hipped androgyny.
His camera's their connecting eye,
the Nikon loaded for the shoot,

as though converting flesh to imagery's
the closest substitute for touch.
He's a style supremo, turned fidgety,

love in the air like ripe guava,
testosterone count risen in his groin,
pouting for the diffident star,

as though he's seventeen, not sixty-eight,
bored with The Quiet American,
and nervous, like he's waiting on a date.

ELEGY FOR A POLKA DOT SHIRT

Unreconstructed 60s
ostentation snowed on blue
labelled Jacques Fath, tailored fit,
fished from Retro on a simmmery
cloud hung-over August day,
bought for pop connotations –
high collar with flouncy points,
cotton married to the skin.
Medium size:
        38 cm:
structured for a defined waist
sexless to the vanity
of ownership.
Affordable at £15,
the item begged me to retrieve
its showy staginess.
        Outside, airless haze,
W11 backpacking crowds
random like footage spilled into
a documentary.

Later I tore a fragile seam
tracking towards left underarm,
the fissure sounding like hot oil
pronouncing itself in a pan.
The tear backtracked through history
to the anonymous wearer,
who bought sensation, sold it on
into a chain, the onion skin
thinning from use;
        the scar re-sewn,
but evident, a little glitch
caught in the fabric like a blues
lament,
the singer head-bowed on a stool,
cooking up trouble, while the club
tug at his vulnerability
and modulate applause from hot to cool.

SWINGING LONDON

Two gay boys slip out of a Soho loo.
The law still squeezes like a python's grip.
They speak polari: one has a tattoo

dangerously visible to the decoy
hanging out underground all afternoon.
He's butchly feminine. A pretty boy.

London's villages synergise the beat
as a collective groove – it's in the air –
the speed of light travels under the feet.

Hockney's in town, his aqua swim-in blue
changing forever how we see water.
His technicolour turquoise comes up true.

The changes happen fast, metabolised
irregularly, like a B complex
kicking in power when it's least realised.

Pink Floyd go ballistic at the UFO,
their stratospheric Stratocaster overkill
injecting mania into the light show.

The Waste Land's synchronised to catchy pop,
Eliot and Hendrix panned through one speaker.
Kit Marlowe waits at the 14 bus stop.

The rain is happier for being rain.
Poetry's in the undertow; the word
keeps reshaping itself for a refrain.

Harrods seems less a barracks. Biba's in.
The epoch burns off rudimentary fat.
Kafka's its archetype: mosquito-thin.

The gays boys separate at Broadwick Street,
resume their double lives, as thunder builds
like scaffolding around the solid heat.

THE DEALER

Lean, and headed Sherwood Street –
B-side of Piccadilly's node,
his fuchsia-tinted glasses screen
London's grey Rothko monochrome,
its subtext rain and rainier
presentiments in June.
His hooky
Dylanesque terminology
has overdosed on Blonde on Blonde,
his rose-flecked floral shirt's labelled Lord John.
He's anonymity: the man
inside and out The Man
who never stays, and deals
by sleight of hand.
Acid, speed and DMT,
no bad cuts, are his currency,
insidiously moving through
the crowds as a virtual body,
a post human fade-out, a bleached
discontinuous identity.
Jamie's his contact; a speed freak
band entrepreneur, stylish Mod
clubber at the Marquee,
who's never late, his money clean
inside an envelope.
He sees him windowed in the same café.
The H users space outside Boots.
Avoid. Avoid. His stash is sealed
inside an album's cardboard sleeve –
the unsuspicious gift he'll make
to Jamie of the Small Faces'
Ogden's Nut Gone Flake.

MODS

An edgy, narcissistic cult,
a group assembled in Ham Yard,
sharp-suited, clothes obsessed
to minutiae of button shapes:
Soho's their patch, when blocked on pills
purple hearts, a.k.a. Drynamil,
SKF granules engineered
for cool, speedy euphoria.
Carnaby Street aficionados
in striped blazers, knife-seamed hipsters,
candy-coloured button-downs,
hair fixed by invisible lacquer,
they're a scooter hegemony,
teenage fashion sophisticates,
clubby, tight-knit misognyists,
neat, cute and immaculate.
They burn to live and live to burn
on optimal R & B;
their bands detonating the floor
with punky energy,
the snappy Small Faces and the Who
at the Lyceum and Marquee.
They're style elitists, up all night
at the Flamingo, out at dawn
pirating market-stalls for thrift
a box jacket or snakeskin boots,
mirrors for a Lambretta stack,
obsessive in their serendipity,
fading the moment, high on it,
flooring the kickstand, horneting
a silver bike to Stamford Hill.
Their youthful coup's all self-destruct,
an auto-combustive signal
to blaze brightly for a few years
jacketed in a union jack,
and take no prisoners, least of all themselves,

but disappear, as though the lot
took off, and migrated into the night,
and kept on, without thought of turning back.

THE MERSEYBEATS

The quiet ones, frock coats and frills,
'I Think of You' a ballady
snowball amongst strafed decibels,
a peppermint cream sound, tempo
dissolving like dark chocolate
on the tongue.
Their songs are love letters written by chords
stretched lazily the way a cat
compounds its yoga to a ball
of tabby somnolence. 'Don't Turn Around'
sleepwalks its way from Liverpool
to vamp the air-waves, frothy style
spilling lace on the charts.
They're soft like a blue velvet cuff,
tooling romance from dockside origins,
finding a way to reach the heart
and shape a song to settle there
as a red sequinned fit.
Their accent's thick as epitaph,
posted into the song like a ship's name
glowering above the harbour berth,
a vocal trademark.
'Wishin' and Hopin'' twinkles with regret,
as though love's better kept top shelf
like clear gold honey in a jar
sealed from the enquiring spoon.
Short-lived, un-adaptive to change,
they lost out, got jettisoned in dry-dock,
another act in pop's unending mortuary
of casualties – three hits a rocky end
the future sealed up like an envelope.

ASA BENVENISTE

The thin one. Belsen, Dachau-thin,
black T-shirt under a silver
cashmere V neck:
your voice smoked from Camel filters,
a quiet New York inflected baritone
resonant as Leonard Cohen's

phrasing from a thoracic well,
each word selected for its body weight
in gravity.
You wore a Saturn-shaped blue opal ring
like a poem, sparkly planet
drawing the eye to its slow-burn pulsar,

my first impressions circa 1970,
a foghorn blowing growling sax offshore,
you flying in and out that day –
here for my burn-up poetry
you claimed had a leopard's heartbeat
inside its detonative imagery,

a flavour, just like Rimbaud, so you said,
in hallucinated intensity.
You wanted twenty-five for a first book
from Trigram; you the handsetter
raising ink off the page like a cobra,
its bite into paper so clean,

you felt the raise like black nail gloss
as the printer's signature.
You were London's small press cult publisher,
bringing me books – Raworth, Jim Dine,
injecting trust in me to have my hand
walk like a shoeless nomad on the line

I still keep now. You ate yoghurt
instead of meals, and got race circuit highs
from volatile Turkish coffee,
published outsiders with impunity,
worked at your own poems, a Jewish rite
of fetching kabala to verbal chemistry,

and had the tree of life tattooed
in black and scarlet on your nape.
You got me to London. I owe you all
the shape-shifting miles I've tracked on the page.
You died an amputee, your left leg stumped
like Rimbaud's, eaten by diabetes

and gangrene.
Your chess partner was a whisky bottle
progressively losing out its level
to your tried hangover immunity.
Your last poems were like morning glories,
lyrical, blue, scented like the Tangier

you'd lived in 1953.
I see you still, the foggy day we met,
me naïve, disingenuous, and you
already my instructor, thin blue jaw,
saying half in humour, but more in truth,
poets only live by breaking the law.

MARY ABSALOM

The tidal drop was 40ft,
the shore like a postcard from Mars
sent across 105 million miles,
you mixing a mule-kicking martini
for a space programme in our cells,
red Oreal hair, black YSL dress,

ubiquitous black, your trademark
invariable signature.
You were my surrogate mother,
a feisty diva turned psychic,
a medium to big shots, the Guinnesses,
corporate hoi polloi with flaws,

speculative venture capitalists.
Your first floor was my sanctuary,
a window open on the bay,
the sea a murky aquamarine,
we sitting listening to Lou Reed
narrating X-files on a Factory queen,

the night arriving, inkjet black,
a star-shot slab over the coastal towers.
We were each other's stimulus
for my post-grad vacations home,
my head full of John Ashbery
and leftfield New York Francophiles

disrupting lyric rationale…
Your birthmark fascinated. Upper lip
twisted with a rhomboidal splash;
our anorexic phenotype –
you 6 stone and me barely 9
of hyperactive energies,

had us share clothes for nocturnal
forays into the Side Door bar,

its underground gay milieu
exploding across the dance floor,
a strobe light tracking silver walls
with a pink holographic star…

Your loss was Johnny. The rent boy
you'd shared a flat with in Queensway,
a platinum meat-rack raconteur
who filled you in on every scene
from nude cleaning with a feather duster
to pick-ups underneath the street.

You gave me taxi grants, brokered
my belief in extravagance,
and are my rôle model today
for living in the moment, fast,
immediate, juicing the page
like the hard shoulder of the motorway…

You sold the house and moved away,
relocated to the city,
the two of us dispersed across
the metal jungle's anonymity,
you East, me North, the divide felt
as abstract, unquantifiable loss.

We lost each other through the years,
hurried down windy corridors
that open on the universe.
Age, you would say, is like a helium balloon
defying gravity?
My mind keeps coming back to you,

the story incomplete, you gone,
but backlit in my memory,
head slightly thrown, small mouth exclamatory
with life's surprises, the harbour backdrop
framed in the window, the violent sunset
like hara kiri drenching a white shirt.

PAULA STRATTON

I come to meet you twenty years too late,
Temazepam spilled all over the bed
like a pearl necklace shattered on its string
at Chester Gardens, you already dead,
your red curls stabbing the white sheet,
your books and things, *The Glass Bead Game*,
scattered around you, and your goblin ring

now turned dispassionately cold.
You died at 28, your overdose
a last defiant act of liberty,
the lonely, drug-crammed exit that you chose
irreversibly final as the door
locked on a Boeing at take off.
You'd left a jigsaw puzzle on the floor

of Tolkien's Journey through the Middle Earth,
the pieces scattered as component bits
of your fragmented, incomplete journey.
The man you loved, your dealer, was the pits,
blue sunglassed speed-freak Dave, banged up inside
for selling rafts of dodgy LSD.
You couldn't break his strangulating hold

on your emotions, or the drugs he fed
your confused, chaotic dependency.
I used to stay with you at Strawberry Hill,
lie in your attic mapping poetry
and synchronise our love of small detail
by looking at an oak leaf or snowflake
until we'd transformed the thing totally

by trading likenesses, a visual game
best qualified in autumn, when the street
swam with the violent clutter of silk leaf.
You had no place in life, each new retreat

a friend's room, or a space found on the floor
invested with your aura, like the sun
had risen indoors. Once I heard your name

called out behind us at Piccadilly,
and it was Dave, and you were gone again
to his white powders and mean underworld,
his dirty money dampened by the rain.
You were so pure, and he the opposite,
but couldn't help yourself. You clung for life
to what he gave you, raw, injected pain.

You the idealist, never had a job,
but waitressed periodically, and were
insider to a vision you explored
as your reality, a journeyer
who lyricised a dream. I see you still
in a red velvet coat in Richmond Park
dancing between the trees, arms open wide

like their forked branches overhauling breeze.
Your letters reached me in their naïve hand,
round as an apple, written in transit
chasing a festival for a hot band…
They'd arrive as effusive fat packets
twinkly with drawings, you'd seen the Pink Floyd
playing so high they seemed to stand in trees…

The breakdown came before you faced the end.
Dave hurt you so hard he was like a wall
you ran against, each rejection harder
until the pain itself wasn't the fall,
but how to live with it and still want more.
Your disappearances grew more prolonged
as though you'd stepped into a corridor

with all the lights out in the underground.
You had it planned of course and took a place
in which to die, and personalised the room

and chose your moment, leaving not a trace
of negativity in words you wrote
your mother and young sister, raying out
your orange sunny feelings in a note

that never once conceded to despair
and trusted in the pills as a clean end
and kept the light on as a comforter
as though it was a last indifferent friend
against the final dark, and died that way
not knowing where to go or who you'd be
beyond the ordinary London day?

JOHN BERGER

An 82-year-old Marlon Brando,
your hair dyed beach blond, sandy gold,
effusive to the velvet coat collar,
you drove a fire-red Alfa Romeo
convertible, a scorching shape-shifter
burning the bendy coastal road

as though you were still 23,
not broken, stringy as an Afghan hound
circling its own tail like the tree
it's chosen as a place to die.
You lived on bananas and insulin
and Cooper's smoky Lapsang Souchong tea,

mismanaging your diabetes
with KitKats, chocoholic sugar hits,
and going off-map searching for a vein
to stick the needle in. You never slept,
afraid that if you did you'd die,
and sat up all night, staring out to sea

wrapped in a blanket, a lighthouse
signalling like a white slow-burn quasar.
You stashed your properties with junked antiques,
the pile up like a looter's hoard
of scrambled treasure gutted from bank vaults,
a four million pounds legacy

dispersed by Christie's at your death…
You had your mother mummified
in a glass box – it scared me cold –
the incest you confessed, her being there,
her bandaged body wrapped in white and gold,
the house lights on all night, the bare

bulbs throbbing like conical eggs,
opalescent planets stalling the dark.

Your pet crow, Topsy, gobbled cheese,
legging it on your shoulder, broken wing
spread like a shattered umbrella,
feathers black as a funeral car.

You were the guardian of hurt animals,
but not yourself, a Great Dane, twenty cats,
a barrel-bodied Labrador
called Nimbus, with a black halo,
that used to lick the convalescent crow
hopping to gain advantage on the floor.

Your eccentric misanthropy,
I swallowed it like a drug at 20,
and saw in you the perverse saint
flaming in my aberrant cells?
I was the witness to pathologies
burning you out, the crazed delusional

obsessions flaring up at 2 a.m.
that you'd been poisoned, off the wall
paranoia that you were really two,
your double waiting for you in the hall?
Death seemed so close, it smelled like car leather
upholstering your biffed vintage Daimler…

Your voice, I have it on total recall,
the tentative stammer, the fractional
delay in connecting two thoughts
as though a gap in the circuit
had forced apart the carriage and the train:
a voice so quiet it had me concentrate

on each inflection and retain
the sentence like an undulating fish
still browsing fins up in my memory.
You'd made friends with the German Commandant
in the occupation, 1940,
and sold him antiques, your duplicity

rewarded with good wines, the swan
you dined on in burgundy sauce
while the populace grew endemic thin.
Years later, you had a house torched
by arsonists, who left a gutted shell,
and tagged your car with Nazi graffiti –

Heil Berger for the Iron Cross…
Your live-in assistant was 23,
Glenise who loved you like a rope
bunched into convoluted knots.
You, the starved elephant were impotent,
your yellow tusks dropped on the ground,

your mind working to substitute
a tricky metaphysic for your loss
of libidinal frequency.
I watched resentment twist your life
like hara-kiri done with slow
positionings of a blunt knife,

the pain prolonged as mental agony…
It was the dark you feared, black 4 p.m.
in December, crushed strawberry light
swallowed into a purple slab,
your fear building around the night
as regenerative insomnia,

the brain too fired-up on alert
to ever shut its streaming imagery.
No pills worked on your chemistry,
no consolation reached you then
in your exhausted state of anomie,
as though your body was a common hurt,

each place occupied like your mind
with pain that never conceded to sleep.
I wrote all your admissions down
for a defunct, interrupted memoir,
a book pulled from the underworld,
the monster holding up its bloody paws,

the struggle incomplete and desperate.
Glenise lit fat cigars and fumed
at your irascible demands –
your phobic descent into starvation,
a banana a day, or late-night chips
picked at from Sizzles, too soggy, too fat

to coax a ruined appetite.
You wore a desert-coloured cardigan,
a Great Lake in a diamond ring,
and called your house sparrow Catullus
and had the little poet sing
eventfully inside in an open cage

at Tivoli, the house you named
after your mother's habitual resort,
the walls washed fluently by marine light.
I wondered at your impetus,
your resistance to death, the short
catch of breath sometimes at your heart

and just how deep your secrets were contained
like a great oak's defiant roots
acquainted with a site 500 years.
Glenise slept in the bath for lack of space,
contorted, wrapped in a fur coat
beside her discarded black suede knee boots…

I drank or piled in the roomy Daimler
for late night policing of your properties,
a bottled window, no alarms,
an avalanche of books crashed in the hall,
you knew each place as mental geography,
a contents mapping, clear, precisional,

the only light in town a pharmacy's
mint green lettering jumpy in the rain.
I heard your loneliness above
your quiet – you absorbed the night
like pigment colouring your memories
as black on black. We spoke of heroin

as a terminal palliative
or anything that killed a nerve
connecting to a German officer,
your mother, death, your loss of potency,
and tried to find a dealer by the port,
our car conspicuous as an embassy's,

the rain endgaming atmospherics on the roof.
You wanted youth, I wanted age,
you wanted life, I wanted death,
the tragic contradictions so acute
it brought us together; the docks gone dead,
the darkness pushing at us palpably,

your life brought to this final edge
of wanting coffee more than anything
for human comfort in the cold.
You spoke of your mother's gold wedding ring
worn on your little finger. A ship's horn
toted a lonely resonating wail

like jump-starting consciousness from a dream.
That signal seemed a link towards your end,
as though you'd been called out to sea.
Autumn turned smudgy in orange valleys.
You wouldn't eat, turned thin like fog
as your dispersing energies

turned to inconsequential things
as a distraction. Drips and tubes
maintained a chemical efficacy
reorganising you, so you could die
less frightened now the morphine overtook
anxiety. We had you try

composure as the state in which to drift
away, but you resisted giving in
to loss of personal identity
and pulled back from the edge each time
like someone troubled by air pocketing
who holds the armrest for support

over a violent squally Atlantic.
Two days, displaced inside a nursing home,
your descent went into free fall,
no bottoming out, you were bone,
the rattle in your throat a castanet,
the dying hard and tangibly brutal,

you drowning on your own fluids
as though a knee flattened your chest
before the frantic breathing stopped
like a car alarm menacing the street.
You'd gone at last to the interior
as a place where all converging roads meet

without direction. In the final heat
they burnt you with your mother to clean ash
liquidating dodgy genealogy.
We waited outside in the fogged valley,
the oaks gummed by grainy November murk,
the raw damp chasing us into a pub

to pick at words that didn't fit
your person, and outside two rainy crows
stripped a ham sandwich, wrestling the fat,
and we quietly turned over memories
like cloud patterns we'd taken for granted
breaking up now and trailing out to sea.

MERCY

Mercy's their leader, ex-Harrod's food hall
cheese counter trainee, size 20,
addicted to purple and triple-decked
cheeseburgers floored between two military helmet-
shaped buns: fat: 75g,
energy: > 1000 cals + French fries.
Her HQ's a disused Vauxhall gym,
licked purple, and her ninja bodyguard
fanatical as Mishima's Tatenokai.
They pump the brain's reward circuit with fat,
disarm the hypothalamus
with leptin excess, sugar, carbs,
Mercy and 30 clones, bashing one-seater jeeps
along the Strand, a purple cavalcade
declaring war on thin.

      She modelled for Vogue,
researched the brain's dependency
on its own opioids, appointed an army
of hypogenated XXLs,
and stoned the swimming pool with freefall dives,
the water thrashed by tonnage to white smoke.

The thin grew thinner under threat,
choreographed themselves like laser beams
across the de-accessioned cityscape,
their arterial elasticity
a winner. When they dematerialised,
like air traffic wiped from the computer,
Mercy celebrated with kobe burgers
varnished with champagne mustard, rampaged out
to the North Circular, gunning for thin,
her convoy armed with machine guns,

and returned to Vauxhall, a new leader,
pummelled by black masseurs, her size

increased to 24, her guards
dancing mini-earthquakes in tow,
her fridge stocked up like a mausoleum
with sides of beef, ostrich and buffalo.

WEST END SURVIVAL KIT

My canvas stash bag kitted out –
Evian water, Rescue Remedy,
more seriously pharmaceutical
Propananol
to slow racy adrenaline:

potentised Melissa granules
for nausea, a Nokia,
a digital Nikon
for snapping Asian boys and girls
mutantly cross-pollinated

with chic high street fashion.
An i-Pod for transmitting pop,
black aviator sunglasses,
3 Pentel sign pens, a notebook,
a pot of Solgar St John's Wort,

each capsule shaped like a nose cone
packed with hypericum.
Organic Brazil nuts for snacks,
a banana for slow release
blood sugar energies,

an A-Z for referencing
streets like the billions of brain cells
highwayed across the matrix.
A bottle of Creed
Vetiver as comforter

for thin skin vulnerability,
I cross the West End zone aware
of dirty bombs, petrocarbons,
hallucinate a blinding flash
of fire ripping through Soho Square,

and keep my cool, as sunlight films
familiar landmarks, hypes the day
with slow dazzle, like clear thinking,
me out and soaking up the crowds
this nervy shopping Saturday.

ALTERED GEOGRAPHY

He shows me a silver foil ownership:
a moon plot pinpointed on a moon map
the bright side grid 1103,
a Safeways purchase: £12.99,
if he can make weak gravity,

do rehab in no atmosphere.
He wants to be a black masseur
at the Lunar Hilton's facilities,
tells me his dream on Shaw Street, window up
on the King's Road toxicity,

a shy, window-boxed, deep red cyclamen,
fleshy as ear lobes, holding on
through nurture to the urban scene,
the claret spearhead flowers tutelary
to somehow thinking green . . .

We shift topography closer –
Henry Becks doodle – the tube map
plotted in 1933 –
lines vertical, horizontal,
or 45 degrees,

the river the only surface feature,
width of a blue bra strap and kinked
like a tagliatelle strand,
the diagram remapping space
London as psychogeography –

Watford moved in like a chess piece,
the suburbs suddenly players.
Our city. But we're lost in it,
above, below, endless repeat:
no way out of its corridors

replicating our arteries.
We take appearances on trust,
your moon plot in its foil wrapper,
there in your wallet : the King's Road
rumbling like thunder in our blood.

SMART PILL

He's ex-Memory Pharmaceuticals,
Chanel leather trainers, the double-C
visible like a DNA helix,
the mapping of a logo gene.
Debriefed in the pharmacokinetics room –

he throws curves at pilots for CREB pathways
inside a Cessna flight-simulator,
his London floor plate a drugs corporate
ledged in the Canary Wharf obelisk.
Off-message, he's obsessed with fear of death,

imagines it as the Blackwall tunnel,
a corridor into an atrium
conferenced by execs in head bandages.
His candidate drug targets Substance P,
works at de-routing it from receptors,

the highways plotted on the brain atlas.
Sometimes he stares into the empty sky,
as though the future's waiting in reverse,
and he's no longer linked to time, looks up
and retrieves the detail of a tail fin…

Recreationally, he shoots crash-test dummies
in the company's soundproofed gallery,
mashes their craniums, or goes somewhere
East of Commercial Road to a dungeon.
The drug he uses wipes the memory.

He's Luke, and shares his life with a python
kept gorged in a convex vivarium,
a custom-built pyramid, family seal
and cryptographic motto goldleafed on
an artefact resembling a Cornell.

His wager's that he'll eat it: python steak.
Shoot it himself and do the autopsy,
then slice it for the freezer. It's perverse
the way he rubs the gun tonight on scales
and tells himself to count backwards from ten.

THE RECKONING

Vaughan's pilot's jacket's bruised like old rhino.
His portable fuel cell for a lights out
goes backpacked on the underground.

He cabs over to Eaton Square.
The Ray-Banned driver's dressed in combat gear,
a holstered automatic underarm.

He transcribes genes, downloading every cell
into a software-based facsimile,
and is genome decoder to the stars –

Kylie Minogue, Madonna's mitochondria,
knows their cellular errors, keeps it all
a confidential lingua franca.

He visits Viv who has the photographs
of Princess Diana alive in Cannes,
a foot shorter, twisted anatomy,

recontextualised scar tissue concealed
by skin-graft surgery.
Her Emporio Armani T-shirt's

boosted by silicone. Security
sights her from a black Mercedes.
Viv has her Diet Coke can for samples.

They sit on Japanese-style stools.
The drought persists. Outside, an orange sun
fries hazy petrochemicals.

H.R.H. has a contract out
on this blonde afterlife simulacrum:
Di as an endlessly repeatable clone.

Vaughan knows he's watched. The Jeep outside
has on-board machine-guns, a snoop
positioned in it with a cold black eye.

YUKIO-JOE AND PRINCESS DI

The Wagamama seafood takeaway
is picked at like a game of chess
played with red frilly octopus.
Yukio-Joe's stick-on video patch
worn on a charcoal cashmere sleeve
is messaged by a tribal friend –

Princess Diana back again
dodging CCTV at Harvey Nicks,
her face retooled after the crash,
her brain still part amnesiac,
she's deactivating a black Moschino dress –
her grabby kleptomania

an outtake from her cryogenic freeze.
London/Tokyo's one city,
its cultures fused, their corporates
recredited by virtual air.
Di wants to meet in St James Park,
the lesions still show through her hair

from an impacted cranium.
Her video jewellery turns from red to blue
prospecting meeting with a friend.
Her credit's dodgy, zeroing.
She's downloaded good genes into
an android replica

and drives a six-cylinder DB5
with touch-screen onboard weaponry.
Yukio-Joe tweaks the toe hole
of a pageable orange sock.
He's Di's post-big-freeze confidante –
a psychocryogenic therapist

cool as a sleepy blue diamond.
Di's red hair's like a Greek poppy.
She shakes from a dysfunctional
Seroxat implant, balls the dress
and sashays to the driver's seat.
Yukio-Joe Ferraris out

through irate taxis to the park.
Di's waiting and she's in a mess,
hallucinations streaming through her brain.
She's got it bad, withdrawal from fame.
Her red hair fidgets in her eyes,
it's coloured like a strawberry stain.

He falls in step under the trees.
Today he's linked up with a gun.
Buckingham Palace is burnt down.
She's manic, edgy, panicky,
video patches signalling, puts on
black shades and stares into the sun.

DRUG GIANT PA

The brushwork in her blackcurrant toenails
looks scored by
a rotating abrader.
She tweaks a Jimmy Choo slingback
into position, rocks her foot
coercively, keeps clicking on to track

a weblink to Cancer Research UK.
Her i-Pod feeds her Britney Spears.
Her floor's that high she sits in clouds
soaped by their immigration.
Her building's a lean-to glass shard –
a black mirror toothbrush stood vertical

over Canary Wharf.
She doesn't think of nose cones crashing through
as a Fundamentalist incentive.
Someone's got the dangling hexagonal
molecule RAD51D
under scrutiny for cell death

like a registration number
on a top security Jeep.
She's paid to disinform. Each day
she dips into a glass-tiled swimming pool
under the city, purifies
herself in a flame-orange bikini,

steams the corruption from her skin
in a same-sex Jacuzzi . . .
They'll do it one day: spike drinking water
with a fat-soluble toxic cocktail –
she knows the formula
for slow, endemic genocide . . .

The data orbits in her blood.
She tubes across the city screened
by dark glasses, and exits at Regent's Park.
The migraine's back like neural spam
policing her nerves. Her blue funk mood
stays with her indoors, sitting in the dark.

JAFFA CAKES

It mattered outside – pink hydrangeas –
a lipstick pink bleeding to mauve and blue
pumped up by iron, like steroids,
and that your black iPod was branded Zen,
a compact Chinese alien
loaded with Turkish pop, and that the day
was Sunday in the rubber universe
and that we sat out back before the rain
banking ideas – I want to be
an image banker, selling corporates
access to colouring facts with imagery,
giving thought-patterns notes, contours,
an individual edge, a quantum leap
out of the grey room into the blue
oxygenated imaginative reality.
And Jaffa cakes, it mattered too
you chose the third and fifth selectively
by looking to negotiate
a symmetry, 38mm
chocolate layered over orange jelly,
54mm diameter,
1gm of fat – I need the specifics
of this McVitie's masterpiece,
a slim-line bite we crunch by scaffolding,
you telling me that the Black Sea's
a deep turquoise – I choose the first and last
as my endgaming do or die
three-layered tangy sponge finality.

VERTIGO

Your airbus thrust for Tokyo –
I'm nervous all day, blasts of vertigo
pocketing me inside our flat:
one holed pink sock, one mauve mismatch
alerting me to the contrast
of feet as art objects

confectioned into colour bands.
I'm liquid nerve for your 12 hours
pressurised in the white skyways
operating a DVD armrest
or tracked by alcohol
whooshing inside your head like altitude.

Spring's here with its camellia spill.
At 17 in love with Bert
(his stammer would have peaked on Tokyo)
camellias rained into my eyes:
hearing him try for rho rho rho
rhododendrons, an April fact

come bursting on the garden
the cerise flowers like Campari
stunningly gunned open.
I do my e-mails, click global
for Tulsa or Nagasaki
as though I moused telepathy

across the digital village.
My fear of long-haul keeps me here
shaping a poem in a capital
highjacked by ministerial czars:
warlords with nerves like smoking guns
power-locked into bullet proof cars…

Our resident black woodpecker
headcrest like a Red Indian's
dips into spray. You're bound for Narita
full on, while our agile black jewel
stays on my eye a moment flickering
a white feathery tiara.

THE FUTURE ARRIVED TOO EARLY

A beach-house by a green lagoon;
the sea ploughs iambic pentameters
across global effluvia –
condoms, computer discs, an aircraft seat
blown out of a crashed Boeing,
a Kylie love-doll beached and sat

legs open in a striped deck chair,
a porno-clone that's up for grabs,
the detail so good, that she's real...
The couple live there in a speeded-up time,
he's a blue sky ufologist
and she a Euro-Thai

abductee
reading a Martian tourist guide
in a black string bikini:
details of a humanoid autopsy
coded into the CD tucked
inside a ferric-orange cover.

He injects the hormone
thyroxine:
(efficacity unproven).
He's back from Area 51,
head full of alien visitations
and rock-storms blown out of the sun...

He looks out over junked debris –
an old army amphibious Dodge truck,
a crocodilian landing craft.
The army's inland, locked in Vietnam?
frozen in time, the jungle crystallised
to components of LSD?

He waves to Rudi. She lifts out of time
for 30 seconds and stares on,
her body a holographic insert
in the bleached day. She's very cool,
then reverts back, hair turned breezy,
her shoulders covered by his strawberry shirt.

TIPPING POINTS

Magnolias collapse like a pink trifle,
a mashed dessert, get flattened underfoot
in cold abrasive thunder showers. I feel
the planet air-pocket in spin
like a plane thrown about by wind
somewhere above the China sea,
the passengers starting to crawl with sweat.
It's a race between tipping points,
a switch to sustainable technology
or collapse: a network blackout,
all power crashed.
One school holiday, lost in blue mirage
hazing the beach, right down on the green tide
a friend grabbed a rubbery octopus
out of its niche, in a rock corridor,
tentacles grabbing, and its black ink cap
projected over his white shirt,
the stain opening out like a continent,
a sort of blackest Africa.
It's the shock I remember, the black squirt
gunned like a missile launcher, and my friend's
momentary shattering against a rock.
It's my three-button black Jaeger blazer
brings it all back, so too the planet's flip
one side light and the other dark,
but angry, light-polluted and burnt-out,
things getting rocky, as I track
across a pink magnolia littered park.

PICCADILLY BONGO

New to the city's nubby underworld,
circa 1982, I'd bongo
with apprehension outside Boots,
or search the honeycomb of corridors
beneath the street, neither for sale
nor picking up, but polarised

to the Piccadilly glut –
bravura make-up, and so thin
I looked a Giacometti,
my buffed red fingernails glossy
as a black cherry.
Got propositioned all the time

by strangers in the underground,
their strung-out, urgent flip-side-up
obliqueness of tactics, part fear,
part desperation, high on risk
and big crowd anonymity.
Met in that way on the stairs down

an address book of blue eyes, palpably
coated in loneliness, like chill
walled on a bottle dug from freeze.
Kept going back, and couldn't break
compulsion all summer, and saw
stand in the ginger light a regular,

sniffing the Soho grid at 6 p.m.;
black glasses, black Gestapo coat,
an ostentatious fugitive
tracking a scent, age overdubbed
by electric aura –
70-50 aggregate?

a man separate by his identity,
I recognised as the louche Grand Guignol
of pigment, the gangsterish, street-wired
Francis Bacon, taking time out
as a quizzical spectator
leaning above the subway gate.

30 BEDFORD SQUARE
for James Lasdun

Your cluttered office, 30 Bedford Square,
the 1980s like a champagne cork
impacting an abrupt trajectory –
you looking like James Dean, your hair
structured like his, but wavier,
cool with the lived-in flash prerogative
of 25? You were my star-turn editor

who wrote like Nabokov, each line compact
with sighting an optimal metaphor.
You read my drafts in red Silvine notebooks,
the light brokering rhomboids on the floor,
and taught me how completion is the art
of reappraisal, and a poem needs
maintenance, like a fast Jag overhaul.

I'd come in Wednesdays, diesel in the air,
cooking with carbons on Tottenham Court Road,
into an island, Bloomsbury's solid wealth
there like the Woolfs' and waiting to explode…
Cape was the Maschler epicentre, wired
to virtuoso fiction by his dare,
his astute entrepreneurial frisson

juiced by panache and overreaching flair…
I learnt the little of my art from you
and how immediacy refined by care
fine-tunes a poem's breath, its diaphragm.
Our work complemented each other's trick
of turning sensual imagery into
a visually liberating energy

raying out brightly like a jeweller's star.
I lived on tranquillisers – valium
metabolised to acute addiction,
tubed in from Regent's Park, the underground

riffy with menace in my panicked nerves.
We read Marvell, and his update, Thom Gunn,
and started novels with the same firepower

the cheetah feels in bringing down its prey.
We drank on Dean Street: the French House furore,
hoping we'd smash the club that Burroughs called
Brit Literature, with its thug minders on the door...
You left for New York, I went underworld,
l'enfant terrible, drug damaged, crawling through
four years of residual strung-out withdrawal...

Today I'm steadier, I feel your pull
attract like gravity in what I write,
sitting out on crumbling back steps, the sun
filmic as glycerine in September,
chasing a poem, the red wine I drink
accelerating chutzpah through my veins,

and go inside to read your new e-mail –
you're out in pristine wilderness with bears,
summer beside a mercury poisoned lake?
you boating through clouds, ruminative, alert
to writing possibilities, and how
visceral trout respond towards nightfall
bulleting flies in the red afterglow,

while I return to brash tobacco plants,
their sweet-scented white flowers, and stay outside
trying to get the intractable right,
polish a phrase for you, as time well spent
attentive to detail, and surrender
to lazy radiance, and work with it,
the slow, amazing honey-coloured light.

WHY I HATE POETRY

I prefer Maltesers to poetry,
asymmetrical chocolate moons, they're like
planetary outriders to Saturn or Mars,

crackly ovoids dissolving on the tongue.
I don't know why Brit poetry seems stuck
like a car locked into reverse

churning backwards into the past.
I'm with the present like the newest drug
altering brain chemistry.

Prose does it better. Haruki Murakami.
It gets the detail, like the things girls do
sharing an i-pod or buying paste rings

coloured like marzipan or blue lagoons.
Poetry needs a ritual suicide
a scarlet fry-up like a post-op sunset,

an end that generates a crazy new.
I'm so thin I'd like to leave a window
and touch down in weak gravity

like a re-entry suicide.
The things people do. I once knew a man
fitted a crucifix to a syringe

each time he shot into a vein.
I write to have something fired-up to read
the colour of crushed strawberries.

It's metabolic. So too Maltesers,
and how they communicate sugar hits,
the chocolate slick as a new cricket ball.

CHRYSANTHEMUMS

Bitterish, tail-end of October scent,
yellow as tarte au citron, a soft fist
200mm
if you like them big, Chinese outtake,
oogiku in Japanese, a bloom head
saucer-sized, potted on a grave
like a sunburst, or the white,
crisp as a laundered shirt with fifty arms
and a mustard nipple for an eye.
It's a hard word to incorporate in song,
Marc Almond gets it on 'J'arrive',
(I'm coming) in four syllables, each vowel
filled like a chocolate with praline,
an optimal chrysanthemum lament
like stripping a shirt from the back.
Today, I'm sent raffish maroon,
a tangy cluster hubbing pussy willow
and holly tubed into ox-blood red paper,
a friend's gift from Henry & Williams
020 7435 3876,
a tonic, uplifting, emotional churn
of winter blues inherent in their mix,
I hold like a partner against
my turquoise jumper, refreshed by their chilled
seasonal bushiness, tall-stemmed intruders
I'll take into my life choosing
the right black vase shaped like a funeral urn.

YELLOW IRISES

Mustardy splash
with a purple-chocolate coronet
I manage 8
going on 10
if I'm attentive, spiky flash

loud in unrefreshed London soil
coned in a cracked terracotta pot.
Their yellow silks are kimonos
without a sash
split open by data in light.

I tend them assiduously
as co-dependents, scrolling tongues
I feed:
little extensions of myself
I need

to need.
A Boeing's engine rumble roofs
the air with thunder.
We're all so vulnerable
doing our thing with urban green

coaxing a fritillary,
a fragilely bruised
ixia –
names like poems
jumped out of the airwaves

into flower.
Me, I do what I can
with water, own nothing but words
to recreate the pull
I feel

for yellow irises
flourishing on our bashed back steps
this steamy afternoon
of big events and small
insects in tune.

JERSEY BREAKFAST

Three white clouds tailback outside my window,
treetop shaped like oak summits
they're level with. I contradict
their inert vaporous complacency
with my wired anxiety:
too little sleep, the deficit

leaving me fuzzy – a whiteout
abstract as foggy signatures
filling the bay with grainy stuff.
The road I walk to clear my head
is coded in my arteries –
a granite archway, a slab of beech trees,

a sunken farmhouse La Retraite,
buried in its green ecosphere
and managed now by two black Range Rovers
parked up like MOD cars at the gate.
I'm here two weeks each year: the flashbacks seem
hallucinated in intensity,

as though the past's all edited on film
in scarily exact chronology:
bits of my life sequenced as digital
reminders of a ripped documentary…
One cloud detaches, and three move on.
The sky tells me the colour of the sea.

Back home I think of breakfast. Cooper's tea,
so smoky it brews autumn in the pot,
a lapsang with such chunky wrigglish leaves
they look like skeins of seaweed on a beach.
Toast's my pretext for Ginger Marmalade,
made by Elvina Davey, 'Burra Tor',

with oranges, lemon juice, ginger root,
from an adapted country recipe:
it spikes the palate without being hot.
These are my ingredients for poetry.
I meet the day full on. The windowed clouds
keep matching form with perfect harmony.

FLEET

A black network in London's thalamus,
a landscaped-over solid trawl
licking a trace into Dead Dog Basin,
like a path-lab procedure,
a subterranean autopsy

of body parts in soup, bottles and dogs,
a swirly ooze down to Kentish Town loch
and under to St Pancras,
furred arteries pushing to King's Cross
as cold bacterial soup, a mucky rush

that puddles on the road sometimes
in thunder-rain at Holborn and Blackfriars
in think-bubbles, the river's secret life
come up to be decoded like intelligence
and splashed through by the tube exit,

I'll never know I've walked it home
in squidgy traces on the floor
at South Hill Park like a liquid barcode.
We talk about the river's drop
at the Magdala, drunk out of the rain

in leaf-slidy November, the street
wallpapered over by stripped orange leaves;
and someone claims they've fucked beside its source,
the bottomless pool by the aqueduct
power-pointing into the river

to feel its drive into the underground,
but it's not clear where water starts,
unlike a road, its shoplifting impulse
traffics into a dark gritty corridor.
We stand above it as we talk,

a disturbed system of tunnels and tubes,
aquifers, islanded from the rain,
and I can feel the drop under my feet
into the Fleet pit, as I buy a round
and feel the fourth or fifth light up my brain.

YAUATCHA

A blue light-box, deep sea ultramarine,
an Yves Klein shot with toothpaste blue
(Colgate Oxygen) faces out
on Broadwick Street, a rainy Sunday fuzz
pixellating beadily, a damp glow
grainy Soho 4pm 30/11 chill
we take inside from reflective windows
of Cowling & Wilcox opposite.
(I make adjustments for altered place states
in my sci-fi Soho novel *The Grid*)
and find immersion in 150 teas
and choose a Pau Dragon Orchid, scent
written into the name, a gold sauna
poured in a cup, a steamy tangy trick
turned on the palate – it's your green tea cake –
three leaf-green suitcases pitted in mousse
like baggage angled on the carousel
arrests my eye, an arty rococo detail
designed to tease the bite: the Cantonese
next to us fork venison puffs
and lobster dumplings, slowly, incisively
like surgery, a serious graft
of separating textures, while I stare
out at a 6ft strip of afternoon
leaked in with shop lights, frontage, drizzled smear,
a Broadwick Street industrial grey different
from any other Soho grey
and feel the transient suspense, the last
shot-down blues bled out of the winter day.

SHOPLIFTING AT SELFRIDGES

My thin friend looks exo-planetary,
the off-world type dressed cool by Richard James,
blue space in his eyes like the China Sea

and dodgy like he counted sugar grains
as focus, filtering them into tea.
He tells me nicking's extrasensory,

dark matter glues galaxies together
and what you pull from jumper stacks instore's
third in the pile, or straight off the counter,

what the left eye attracts by looking right.
He recommends do small talk, make things float,
de-tag with a hook piece, his slippery tricks –

and sometimes uses a detacher gun.
A habituated forensic pro,
he looks money, but needs dopamine kicks.

In the black-marbled Selfridges slab,
an art deco commercialised sarcophagus,
he robs like a retail shrinkage bandit:

his thrill's accelerated by the lights,
their drizzled starburst dazzle when he's on,
brain chemicals car-chasing what he sights –

a striped Westwood cardie done as a trick
that dematerialises instantly.
I got that one: he steals to give away

like my best scent, Vetiver by Guerlain.
He's Nick, and even blocked on Naltrexone
can't help it, always that compulsive grab

to subvert order, leave the pile deplete
like it's numerical, odd not even,
and goes off doing numbers down Duke Street.

THE RIGHT HON. JACKAL BLAIR

Insensitive as a mortuary fridge,
a jackal's
asymmetrically psychopathic grin
like killing's chutzpah, meltdown's fun
people stick like eggs to a pan

fried by depleted uranium
under a radioactive desert sun
neon-red as a traffic light.
Blair's the hipster-suited super-killer
the cool czar monetising war

into personalised futures capital.
The burnt, the mutilated don't move now,
nor bacon-rashered Iraq amputees.
The J.P. Morgan commissar's slap's
a flakeover fake tan

sealing his features when he lies
into a harassed orange smear.
He throws handgun body shapes, sticky spin,
like the man who blew up the world
as missile-guided music hall.

The guilt lodged like a bullet in his brain
he can't extract, a toxic leak
like slow-dose polonium.
His look's impassive as an army truck
an explosive self-propelled howitzer.

He's aggro sicko psycho
a blacked-out Range Rover his cell
locked into minders like a gang
of decommissioned brick-faced commandos
maintaining a globe-trotting criminal.

LONDON FLOWERS

These oriental poppies earthed
as scattered outtakes, rough demos
lucked into NW3
shivery silk minis on runway pins –
pink, yellow, orange, blue and red,
they're like randomised confetti
transient saucerians
an anthology of MAC eye colours
in nitrogen-depleted soil.
I give them names like Toyoko,
Masako, Yumiko, O,
Yuan Yuan, a garden harem
cooking Chinese opium.
Ixia and violet iris
lyricise intense moments,
so too explosive azaleas
and a libidinous steamy lily,
a transplant brain from Asia
with a bulb like a shaved cortex.
This marine blue hydrangea's
the colour of the blue deodorant cube
floating in the Gatwick men's toilet,
a sort of deep Atlantic blue
squirted with ultramarine.
Like everything I see they're poetry,
poppies bringing a dusty frill
to capital affairs, a bright
liaison like a thought pattern;
immediate as light checked-in
8 mins travel time from the sun
to reach this wiry leggy cluster
that tomorrow will be gone.

SOUTH END GREEN TOILETS, NW3

Subterranean Victoriana
Joe Orton's cruisy marble-floored bunker
the black and white diamond Viagra shapes
like playing chess on LSD
the white porcelain rococo urinals
Doulton & Co Ltd
logoed like a printed jeans-blue tattoo
a blue typographic agapanthus
London Paisley Paris.
Black pediments, green and cream tiles,
it's a two-entrance corridor
trapped George Michael hanging there
rainy 23/9/2008
a crack pipe and a droopy joint
his pharmaceutical weaponry
cottaging compulsively
claiming through his fazed drug radar
'it's my culture.'
Ten steps down under, it's a submerged space,
a panicky tribal taboo
a macho micro-Congo
of urban warrior torrential piss.
Someone's tracking a silver digicam
over the time-reversed interior
digitising its tonnage to pixels
light as a thought recreating the real.
Outside the disused spinach-green painted
black cab taxi driver's shelter
looks like it's up for use in poetry –
a grab for quirky imagery,
the rain coming on in teardrop patterns
like a paisley throw printed for Liberty.

WORKSHOP

It's the cardboard carton lettered OSPC
black sans-serif stamp interests me
more than the poetry.
10 of us in a room with trial paint marks
an aqua slash a violet rip,
raw strip lighting, a conference-size table,
all women coming on 40,
marriage or big relationships stared down
immobilised by a red traffic light.
Poetry's now the letting go
of mess, constraint, 'he hurt me bad
and left me crying on the stairs
but now I'm almost glad
I'm free,' Christine relates as a postscript
to reading 'Falling Down the Stairs,'
the vertically abseiling imagery
scooped up by forward signposting
like fizzing coke.
                No poem gets things right,
it reinvents the story, puts in bits
otherwise lost, you never know
the things you do until you write them out.
Christine, with the blonde bob and turquoise frames,
and casual giveaway delivery
like effortlessly pouring wine,
you in the group lead by the pain
you've converted into a state
that's matt indigo with a come up shine.

PULLING THE CORK

A slow dig, a ritual spiral,
a DNA helical twist
of metal punched into the cork –
Peter's corkscrew's flaked ketchup red
and oxidised from kitchen jabs,
with rusty arms
like bits of scaffolding
slung over grungy tangy docks.
I get in fast with a Macon Village,
slow with a resistant obsidian Merlot,
the route in an instinctual thing
like keyhole surgery,
the skewed, the fissured, the rammed
that Peter leaves me, coax
to a popped conclusion, a pop
that's incisively ejaculative
and sounds to Peter filtered up a floor
like a red carp breaking surface
on a still pond. Red, white or pink
the way out's always different
in the gradations of the pull
that's moist or dry, the nose sticky
with a concentrated bullet of fruit.
The act's surreal like bottle dentistry
performed under the street in Holland Park,
the glasses upstairs ready for the pour,
clean as I can make it, a red swirl
travelling a fast pathway to the brain.

MADDOX STREET

A year scrunched angularly on the top floor,
a nosebleed-red crane's arm outside
working a reconstructed shattered site,
I catalogued books like playing mah-jong,
with rare editions, handled thumb-stained skins
rubbed pig, deer, cow, human
epidermis from the 18th century,
the light collecting in scattered colours
as atomised sunshine, blue, purple, red
surges of photons immediate
as consciousness, a drill blasting into
a concrete regolith; the windows shook
from the abrasive shattering
like sitting on a fault line: linen, glue,
full cloth and jackets with edge-wear
part of my process playing book striptease
to get descriptions right and books malleable
to handling. I couldn't sustain
interest in data, my futures radar
working a poem intermittently
against typing in facts in quirky rafts
that looked like strings of Beluga caviar.
I collected Maddox Street in my blood,
walked its quarter lunch times as my anthology
of London street surprises caught its mood
on rainy days best, and nurtured a plant,
a left behind guzmania
rewarding me with a triple raspberry star.

ELEGY FOR PAUL LIGHTBORN

White Jamaican Plumstead Paul,
hatted, prettified dodgy rent
working the blowy circular concourse
at full-on Piccadilly Circus Exit 1
circa late seventies, degraded, hurt,
grime on hot money like pigment,

bacterial traces patterned like snakeskin,
our lives crossed disruptive 2009,
you shuffling, puffy with PCP,
holding up on triple combination,
your antiretrovirals doing bits
to re-regulate toxic downward drift:

April, and I'm lost in my Dilly book,
you as my compromised interviewee,
firsthand streetwise bashed-up smoke and mirrors
residual outtake from an outlawed trade,
remembering the lot, each punter's face
and more exactingly just what they paid

and what you did, subverting public space
into a systemised rent arena.
It broke you, each new undercover raid
hauling you off to Bow Street, nights in cells,
later the Marlborough Street Magistrates Court
and always you went back to hanging out

in people's faces – damaged love for sale –
the exhibitionistic effrontery
a part of it, the rest the need to eat
or party in a club. You'd kept alive
the dead man who'd infected you, no trace
 of bitterness, drinking Jamaican coffees

on Pembridge Road, telling me all of it
with swipes of bitchy humour, and certain
you'd do it all again, win and not lose
if you could correct time, re-write the past,
forking a syrup-drenched waffle, 'You know
 the punter's on you and you've got to choose.'

SHARES

Another risk modeller's kamikaze
zeroes into liquidity,
the virtual blinded by light-speed delays
like contact from another star
or hemlines rising and falling,
mini gone optimal micro
like Britney Spears, or dragged back to the knee.
Most futures contracts sit with psychopaths –
bunkered hedge-funders radiating Earth
with guided clusters, depleted uranium,
and a chemical equator –
the northern hemisphere 120 parts
per billion more polluted than the south.
The best investment's always poetry;
there's never any peak to fall,
no estimable catastrophic crash.
September light's like 80 carat gold,
that pure it turns to gold dust in my hand
and lazes there, a virtual UV sheath
like dipping my fingers into gold paint.
The planet rests at tipping point,
its bankers in dispersal to rocky cities
(Beijing, Dubai, St Petersburg),
the sun today a universal gift
cocktailed with stardust, a bright energy
that bumps up orange, purple, blue,
a natural high to the morning glories
effortlessly opening with soundless lift.

HANGING ON

Wind spills the magnolia like a drinks tray
a sashaying hot cerise swirl
like a pink shampoo
in my grainy window out.
These days I hang in disconnect,
a shoe

lacking another shoe
to pair. The more I know the less,
96 per cent of the universe
comes up as blackout dark matter,
dark energy, like unused brain
turned dark side of the Moon.

It's detail I collect obsessively
like counting stitches on a shirt
or looking at the lipstick bleed
left on a coffee cup.
Sometimes I follow a shoe for its heel
or peeks of a red satin-lined footbed

a Christian Lacroix.
Falling apart is hanging on
to little things that personally mean,
a song still going on in my head,
the black forked snake's tongue
on a loose button thread

a smile framed at me in the street
like cutting chocolate cake.
I never write the dead out of my book
or take their numbers off my phone.
Sometimes I punch in numbers for a dead
friend gone, just for the ring-tone's

familiar frequency.
My magnolia does a splashy striptease
littering its purple silks.
I try to get more present in my past,
move on into the day under churned skies
living each fine-tuned moment like my last.

CHARLES BAUDELAIRE, VOYAGE TO CYTHERA — (SEX TOURIST REMIX)

My heart turned over doing crystal meth
beat like a seagull smashed on a cruise ship,
the hull churning under a seamless sky
the current's rip destabilising as drink.

That off-world island, it's a blackened chip
called Cythera, only Dylan's played there
before gigging at sham Eldorado:
you'd think he'd accessed it through a time-slip.

Bob's on the voyage, a white cowboy hat
sealing in shade: a sexy pull comes up,
a floating scent crowding on feel-good chemicals.
The girls in tangas loll there smoking dope.

The island's green with myrtle, heady stuff,
there's boys there too waiting to give good head:
the skyline's soft as a collapsed red rose;
it shows up violet, pink and lipstick red.

The place was once a focus like Bangkok
for selling sex, now seagulls claim it back:
a generation's litter's on the beach,
beer cans, a raft of condoms, a skewed shack,

no five stars, nor topless girls in the coves,
the hippy guru gone into retreat,
her beads and incense and her mantras blocked,
she's turned psychotic staring at her feet…

But as we came up close, sighted the shore
for cell-phone snapshots, scaring off the birds,
we saw above the camp a forked gallows
a crudely improvised immediacy –

and crows were slashing at a ripe body,
spading out sinew, digging out the eyes,
ferociously churning into the brain,
stripping a plump oligarch to the bone…

The eyes were red holes: was it jackal Blair?
The guts escaped into a tumbling coil
the birds fought over: they'd hacked off his cock
and looped his viscera around his feet.

And there were jackals scaring off the birds.
Like answers like; they guzzled body parts
like US soldiers pissing on war dead.
The leader barked out orders to the pack.

We heard news they'd strung up war criminals
around the island, czars who'd ploughed the Gulf
with depleted uranium: this one
was bacon-rashered. Bob sang 'Like a Rolling Stone'

to put a simmer in our downturned mood.
Thrown by the carcass – his torched jeep close by –
I tasted my end like we always do,
confronted by bloody atrocity:

the hedge-funder, his dodgy dossier,
and now the raw invasion, dog eats dog,
in body-snatching revenge: there were two;
his wife was jacked up on the other side.

The sky and sea shimmered in one dissolve,
but really all I saw was red and black–
Baudelaire deconstructing Baudelaire
confronted by mad predatory attack.

We sailed on, but the man's face comes at me
as a reminder self-disgust feeds hate,
they'd dressed him in his black suit and white tie
as though he had a Whitehall dinner date.

PETER'S LAY OUT

One pink rose, snipped from the garden's jungled bush,
two litter petals, three or four
disrupt logistics in a room
mapped out by Peter's OCD,
he can't function if an object's displaced
3 cms from its base
or if a tumbler's left beside the bed
belonging downstairs, it's an alien thing,
an extraterrestrial invading his space
beside the lamp and the Temazepam
rolled as white planets in the palm for sleep.
The blue house on Holland Park Avenue's
Peter's intelligence, a faded blue
No. 22
the numbers vaporised to faded haze.
Even a paperclip's like surplus weight
on a spacecraft, a book left out
or power on a warp or kink
in the system, a sensitive alarm
that's something out. I've been there so often
each second Friday, no fractional change
in placement, order, furniture,
the light trapped there as compressed microsphere
the colour of a green lemon.
Each room's a zone in Peter's brain,
the hippocampus, hypothalamus,
the limbic seat for piloting the ship.
A dropped crumb's like a golf ball, shoes removed
for risk of infecting the Persian rugs,
no give or take, Peter's bad foot
elevated on cushions, the traffic
drumming the double glazing like a fist.

M&S SOCKS

Black cotton body, I like to walk black
underfoot, black at the ankle
like shirt cuffs, heel and toe
7 variants in this pack,
red, orange, blue, yellow, lavender, pink

and purple, horizontal stripes
branded under the colour block.
I like intelligent socks that think
ways forward like sci-fi lycra
tracking by sat nav and so cute

they're art worn flat like foot candies,
a hot pink with aqua contrast
or smoothie lavender surprise
like striptease back home on the boards
shoes left behind, the arena

for exhibitionistic socks
got into angled geometries
cross-legged or doing yoga
on a black-painted floor
rewritten into showy views

they never give in shoes.
Sometimes they look like stripy sweets
for toe sucking, the heels like orange hulls
on ships, a fit of metaphors
like Lego, sometimes they're like cats

with pointed nose leathers
and twitchy on a scent fidget
for contact with reality.
Mostly they bond with my Converse All Star
as black on black fugitives,

toe-puppets doing their own thing
in tropical colours 7/8
my foot size, and it's recreational
this giving them full play to be
two tropical fish detached from the shoal.

RAINBOW COUNTRY

Jersey deposit in a plastic bag –
a mini-beach, black bladderwrack, scrunched grit,
volcanic, quartz glitzy, a winkle shell
that's nipple coloured, bitty, chipped,
an iridescent oyster lid
all scooped and knotted in a Sainsbury's bag

by Christiane to give me back my origins,
I've dumped on a mauve-painted kitchen shelf
between a perky Coleman's Mustard jar
and Fortnum's Sir Nigel's Orange Marmalade
and left there to get a rotting beach smell,
a tangy compost on a meltdown star –

the London I inhabit, meaty czars
and terrorists; and crunches if I squeeze
the contents, nip the orange carrier's ribs,
a crab's claw in there, olive-green pincer,
and eye-socketed cracked nacreous shell,
a mixed-up mortuary bagged at Grosnez –

the beach shelving into ripping green sea
fuelled like it's a stop-off plane. My coast,
the one skyscrapered with eyebrow rainbows
dissolving my teens into a purple glow
still swims molecularly into my blood,
the light prismatic, seven-band, shimmery,

smudged like a girl's thundery eye-shadow,
dispersed sunlight scattering through raindrops,
the red light highest, the blue innermost,
they came on like a marine Las Vegas,
red, orange, yellow, green and indigo
after a shower laid over St Malo

fuzzed into sunburst as a sign I kept
of sometime dazzle, someday poetry,
and get back prodding sweaty green seaweed
lumped in a carrier to know the high
of rainbow country, all that diffused light
doing hallucinations in the sky.

STARBUCKS PITCH

Most iPad entrepreneurs broker there
informally, this cool-look dude
in blue cuffed Levi's, zippered aviator skin
with a fleece collar like a chilled-out czar
sips Caffè Americano
and plots like he's watching a tennis game
in which the ball bounces before
it hits the court, a wave-like quantum freak.
It's the new global conference space
a floating island with teal-blue armchairs
and street windows out on to tomorrow
that's just more colour faded than today
like sun-bleached jeans.
                         I go there most to write
and people-spot: South End Road or St Martin's Lane
for tobacco-brown faux leather sofas
and the scooped insulation they provide
against big-city rush. Blueberry muffins
have mushroom-shaped summits that look like clouds
stacking to a cobalt ruffled Frisbee,
the lemon drizzle cake's like summer snaps
taken in sun-drenched Hawaii.
I write my Starbucks storyline, modern
cyber-stylist facing a mustard wall
one tone yellower than Coleman's,
a novel that absorbs the end of time
as a banal crash – bankers on the run
into the desert, and looking out now
I note after low cloud a dusty orange sun.

HONEY

A spoon's sufficient, viscous floral gold
bee-lifted by worker flower-probes
sugar-addicted buzzy fur
irate as Goodwood reverb
in bitty tumbling blossom,
ended on my blackened toast.
In Highgate once, I lay flat on my back
for Matthew's shoot, his tomb-robbers series
the nameless grave corroded
like a urinal, and there were bees
collecting somewhere with unstoppable
piloted energies, each sugar fix
like doing sex in a frilled corolla.
I roll my honey on to multi-seed
like expanding a sticky teardrop shape
into an asymmetrical island
for a sweet tooth getaway, a drenched crunch
to an accelerated 8 a.m.
Matthew's dead of a pill-crammed overdose,
his photo book expected, and he's there
inside my honey jar each time I raid
its contents, and remember how he shot
me, arms extended, arranged on the ground,
bees droning close-up at my head,
and with each bite I recreate the sound.

BUYING CUP CAKES

At 42 Tavistock Street
a fuzzy drizzled diamond-grey Monday
an L-shaped diagram away
from Jubilee Market's tables of paste –
its exploded brooch galaxy,
I sight the shop painted like a lemon houseboat,
the Primrose Bakery, after three tries
of misdirected whiteout blanks,
(the street always goes missing or I do)
in Covent Garden's tricky mazy map
of streets constructed like a Lego swastika,
and it's my destination, cup cake days
for Toyoko, time out from a two-day affair
with Robert Duncan's poetry,
I'm writing on orange sunshine in its chemistry,
a CA orange as photonic mix
in his spatially visualised lyric,
and debate pastel icing tops,
and choose a lavender speckled with cobalt
and a chocolate dusted with turquoise stars
as confectionary artefacts
I have to manage upright in a box,
navigate back to Chalk Farm without jolts
to decorated cake nipples, secure
white cardboard mini-coffin in my hand
for Toyoko to break the seal
on sexy areolas, cute summits
sprinkled with star-belts, while the rain comes on
glossing the blotchy reds in grounded leaves.

DEATH DATE CUTIE

The spoon stands sentry by the strawberry jam
a compressed fruit Waitrose cheapie.
I probe a chunk like using a helicopter
to peg the washing line, a chunky cone
shaped like a sugared Mars moon.
My death can't be outsourced, it's done solo,
and not branded to sell or be hijacked
by a predictive text fuck duck.
What if I had my own expiry date
date-stamped invisibly on my hand-back
as a gene-coded real time reminder
I've gotta go, one autumn day
with fog bushing the white chrysanthemums
and planes grounded in the damp air,
no Gaultier Classique jacket
breathed on my shoulders. The time's never right
like jam volume in a donut,
but it's precise like a white robot arm
attaching a storeroom module
to the science-labbed International Space Station
slung together as a bashed docking-point.
I've got my moment when the error's due
as a blackout – like the dark side of the moon
as tipping point – I'll love you to the end:
today the hail cracks in like tumbling dice.

MY DEATH SHIRT

A friend's sumptuous legacy –
I keep it hanging under polythene
a customised John Pearse purple velvet
red-stitched affair, a thunder-cloud
with sleeves and blackcurrant lining

measured for Martyn with his cells
piloted by viral kamikaze,
he had six months to live, frothy April
piling on burnt magnolias in the yard
like shattered confection, his life in bits

and wanted out and drew his shirt
as configurative reward in bed
to soak hospital visits in colour
so saturated it blanked illness out
by density, each blood test a frontline

report on cellular war, T-cells down,
the virus nearing the blood-barrier,
his shirt's resistant personality
protecting him from diagnostic scares,
its full-on Meard Street stitchy pedigree

so irrefutably supporting him
it became Martyn when he couldn't be,
the splash associated with his look,
a sort of cranberry-coloured substitute
for punched out dynamic, the accomplice

to dying in a way he could control
propped up on pillows wearing at the end
this blood-hot fetish for the final shot
dispersing pain, and given me
by his sister weeks later as postscript

to Martyn's ashes – a gritty sachet
sealed from his meltdown, and hung up by me
in storage to await my time
if I can wear it as a purple splash
in the last countdown facing a lights out.

HART CRANE'S JUMP

The *SS Orizaba* – white on black
corroded ship's paint: dead on noon
April 27 1932:
Hart's in his cabin, drunk on Cutty Sark,
a sailor's cap raked on his head,
butch, bruised and beaten – it went wrong
the way it does inside a song,
the hurt compressed into a blues
muddy as mixing paint over a drain.
His pull's downward into a sky
that opens up inside the sea,
the centre of his deathbound hallucinated
gravity, the drop
into white water shattering
like an exploded window.
                              Somewhere else
in Cleveland Ohio
his mother shuts a window on the rain
and worries, and she doesn't know
what panics an accelerated flash
of Hart staring at her full on
as though he's back home and demanding cash
for drink and sailors.

He gets to the stern in a dressing gown
and vaults the railing, shivers there,
the momentum so powerful in his mind
it launches his trajectory
into the churning thrashed-out wake,
his skin still bronzed from Mexico.
His mother punches at a blister pack
of Aspirin for a headache scrunching nerves.
Hart's shipped in transit for New York.
It rains in Cleveland Ohio.
She doesn't really want him back.

from WHITE BEAR   AND FRANCIS BACON

Mostly local, the Regent Palace Hotel,
I'm paid to listen and hold someone's hand
a stranger like an alien
selecting me for looks – I understand –
a suit called Alfie (43?),
accountant understudied charcoal suit,
compressed voice toneless as money
the hurt he carried a disaster site
impacted in him like a plane
nosed through a bank, he'd been caught cottaging
in a Piccadilly car park
with Miss Singapore a.k.a. Paul Murphy
and charged with public indecency
faced unmitigating holistic ruin,
a partnership, a refrigerated marriage
chilly as vodka frozen for shot,
routinals hardwired to his nerves
as all he knew and me paid £50
for listening to his terminally resigned
abdication of life, he'd planned it all,
the pills, his wife's weekend away,
the insurance – I couldn't turn it round
a man whose one tropical splash
was Dilly rent – the colour he could buy
on the railings turning his grey
into a red and pink tropical sky
brushstroked by revved adrenaline,
his aberrational orgasmic high
always bought, he'd been going there
twenty years as a fugitive punter
been warned twice for soliciting,
got off, been robbed, rolled, but kept coming back
as an addiction to the place,
the Samsung, Sanyo and Burger King ads
doing their scarlet LED displays
like turning tricks. I listened to him fade

into irremediable despair
before he cried on the pillow, broken
by emotional shattering,
the whiskey floating off his breath like steam
vaporised from a lake, its heavy pull
sucking into oblivion the way
I knew he'd be dragged down by pills
into a place that's vacuum sealed
and only split open by autopsy
as pathological data, his hurt
exempt from all analysis,
so too emotional pain, degradation
and personal loss gone swimming deep
inside his arteries. I never saw
hope go out quite so terminally
and couldn't do the least thing to reserve
the mad accelerated rip
at which it travelled through his chemistry.
I didn't know his name or ask
knowing he'd lie, and his obituary
elude me as a cold sanitised fact.
I went back outside to the light's
saturated photons at Leicester Square
and sat and didn't move an hour and wrote
a poem submerged in a red notebook
I've lost in time

          *   *   *

                                I go
back to my mist-finned island so little,
it's virtual as the coronae
fracturing Venus, or three days away
the moon's concrete coloured mashed regolith
but it's a Boeing surge over
a lapis lazuli channel, one drink
and twenty-five minutes later,
a granite pretzel swims in the window
no bigger than an arroyo,

an offshore, off-brand legitimised cell
a money ecosphere, you have
anonymous accounts for oligarchs,
and a Chinese puzzle of lanes
with sunken farms and manors sealed like forts
into a video-alert
motion-sensored plutocracy,
but there's black butter, and a potato
shaped like the moon, and sensually
rose-scented as a flushed Sancerre,
a taste that's tangy like seaweed,
the skin dusted with minerals
and licked by iodine salinity,
rare as gold nuggets, blotchy ovoids
flipped like black gold out of the April soil
the sky chilly as a freezer
the rain accelerating in a shower
striped like a rainbow, shimmery
from the Gulf of St Malo, rain's in it,
sparkling Brittany rain in potato,
you taste the sky in everything
grows in an island, and by June
the freckled ovals are replaced by royals,
a chunkier more solid taste
of deep earth roots, a retro-spuddy taste
of something just that rootier
and yellower and fully earthed
like a vegetable meteor
dug out of St John's, it's like middle earth
as a manorial parish
a rusty key to its sealed gates buried
under an oak's twisted torso.
I sat there in fluffy blue topaz fog
with Asa Benveniste, spaghetti thin,
black-shirted, moonstone ring, the kabala
mixed in his language, a word-soup
in which the alphabet swam like noodles
that steamed up into poetry,
Asa the maestro printer and poet

the eye that sanctioned Trigram Press,
there to fire gold in my teen poetry,
I was the poet he compared
to Rimbaud with my shook up imagery
and Jagger body, and his voice
pitched through blue toasted Camel smoke
was baritone cool like Leonard Cohen's
a generational 50s chilled out tone,
understated and lyrical,
a voice that unzipped women, it was silk
climbing like a morning glory
to poetry. We sat and crows convened
with their dodgy runic vocabulary
and threw black shapes, leather parabolas
through puffs of fog, the no-colour sky
like tonic drizzled into gin, the farm
a granite block in the valley,
an unworked, off-limits intelligence
secured by a tax-fraudster drugs cartel.
Asa chainsmoked his softpack Lucky Strike
his language doing smoke signals,
nicotine semiotics, he wanted
a book from me, my formative
clotted implosions, hallucinated,
done for sensation imagery,
and I, already neural in my search
to kick poetry into near sci-fi
wrote like dirty-bombing the dictionary
into my face, tattooed with words
stuck to me epidermally
like subjective iron crosses
that glittered with the tacky paste I wore
badged on my jacket in splashes
of ruby, green and nectarine.

KEITH RICHARDS

So laid back, living where his dimension
touches on inner vision, that far gone
he wouldn't notice a black spotting fly
settle on a cheek and a second one

glint as a double beauty mark.
Heroin as an embalming fluid,
a cellular rejuvenator, he's
like Burroughs, a human experiment

in survival. Fortified, whiskey-shot,
the music lines are always tight, the nerves
feel into that non-committal control;
the man lives for the chords he generates,

and is a kind of latter day Crowley,
an adept of a deathless state, someone
who guards somatic knowledge, most alive
confronting stadia; knee boots, jewellery,

fetishistic tinctures of Joy,
hair brushed in every way that's contrary,
the archetypal rock star, maintaining
the image as reality

through so many mutations, Swiss clinics,
and in retreat at Redlands, someone who
finds a centre in the crazy decades.
'I'm dying, but that means I'm living too.'

RONNIE WOOD

The impromptu interventionist slide-emperor
generic London blues his dialect
chord-wrangler stroking reconstructed BB King
into Stones aggro – he's all swoop and dodge
the nifty hipster rude boy front-man brat
doing the song with raw sexual chutzpah
like he'd knock a hyped-up scarlet Ferrari flat.
Ronnie's crow-profile snouts a cigarette
like it's a balance point, some extrasensory
fine-tuning to get balance right, a fag's
blue curly bootlace of drift-smoke. He's there
by default, euphoric obituarist
to Brian Jones, Mick Taylor, virtuoso blonds
dusting a genii's fingerprint on bottleneck
to make indigo arpeggios bleed.
Ronnie's a river bargee, born into the Thames
with boat-speak: water talks like a guitar
blurring boundaries between rhythm and lead
like late Stones meshing strutting back of Mick
and parallel to the resistant human riff's
brushstrokes that colour-code 'Gimme Shelter'
to dystopian flameout stormy blues.
He wears the look: a slept-in dandified rehab
persistence, odd Stone out, but majorly
textured into rock circus – see him run –
stoned, clownish, tricky with dexterity
patching the sound like he's hemming a coat.

SOME DAY

They'll all come back, the missing in my life
as seamlessly reinvented
topaz-eyed Paula dead from overdose
in a jade dress green as the Sandoz S
on a Temazepam box (her exit):
Bill in a blue cotton bathrobe
at grey marble-floored Peninsula Heights
colour of a foggy airflight, Alan
at 80 zipping into a teen leather jacket
140 lbs like me, giving me *Pickwick Papers*
to sell on as a first bound in green oasis,
and my mother unstoppably blonde
in every decade rehabilitated
to the youth she never lost, the glamour
prototype she gave me, they're all compressed
in a psychic packet, Martin in fur
pushing a deadfish-silver Rolls on the Westway
drunkenly exhilarated by Aids
as climactic danger, living it all
to lose it at Phillimore Gardens, comes back
as a bumpy transcript end of the year
like end of a curve – a broken rainbow
over my backyard that won't disappear.

www.ingramcontent.com/pod-product-compliance
Lightning Source LLC
Chambersburg PA
CBHW032019230426

43671CB00005B/135